Get The
Teaching Job
You Want

Praise for the book

'Your new book is grand! The illustrations are phenomenal and the stories that support the process are a great addition. I wish you lots of success with it and I'm thinking it has more applications than teaching!'

John La Valle, President, Society of NLP

Get The Teaching Job You Want

From Self-doubt to
BEING CONFIDENT
in 10 Easy Steps

Tanya Bunting

ISBN 979 869 725 7883

Illustrated by Anita Bagdi
Designed by Goldust Design

This book is dedicated to all of the teachers who want to overcome any fears or doubts, in order to excel at interview and for the rest of their teaching career. And, ultimately to the children whose future they hold in their hands.

It is my privilege to dedicate this book to one of the most inspirational teachers of all, Dr. Richard Bandler, co-creator of NLP; whose unique skills I use throughout this text, in the classroom and with all my coaching clients to initiate success.

And, to Kathleen and John La Valle, whose explicit training, challenge and support, has enabled me to translate the generic NLP skills they teach, to support the interview process.

Contents

Acknowledgments

My appreciation and thanks go to Tina Taylor and Gloria Hammett at the International College of Clinical Hypnotherapy, for their tremendous support in honing my trancework skills; as well as to Tom Phillips and Simon Adamson for the challenge, Simon Foster for sharing his book writing strategy, Nick Hind who coached my own success in the interview process, Rhianna Bennett and the other teachers whom I've been privileged to coach, and most especially the staff, governors and children at the respective schools where I learnt my own recruitment skills.

And finally, to my family and friends for their constant love and support.

Foreword

This book, which reflects the honesty, core values, warm enthusiasm and skills of the author, captivated me to such an extent that I read it in one sitting. Sensitive and deeply reflective, here was the text that I unknowingly needed when setting out on my teaching career and that would have been just the resource I needed when supporting staff in my role as a Senior Leader in a Secondary School and later, Governing Bodies in their search for the ideal Head and other Senior Leaders for their schools.

Tanya, who I first encountered in my role as a Local Authority School Improvement Inspector, is the consummate and caring educational professional whose desire has always been to share her own ideas and skills in the development of the children and staff in her care. This book, part information sharing and part workbook, takes the reader on a personal journey to a better understanding of self, in order to arrive at the point of recognising that crucial match between teacher and the school culture and the young people it serves.

So much of the learning that will be gained by the reader is applicable well beyond the recruitment process itself, in terms not only of self-understanding, but in applying NLP skills and self-hypnosis in future life situations. The chapter on planning and delivering learning opportunities that engage, enthuse and motivate students is applicable to the furthering of progress in any learning context.

Tanya's experience in teaching, school leadership, the development of a brand-new learning environment and the reconfiguration of a very dated one, together with her creativity and love of writing, shine off the page in a book that is accessible to all.

Lynda Clarke

A Note to the Reader

An Introduction to NLP and Hypnosis

Whether you're applying for your first job, your first promotion or a position on the leadership team, the interview process can be a daunting prospect.

Get the Teaching Job YOU Want is a personal development book designed to teach you all the skills you need to apply, prepare and interview well. During the teaching interview process, you're required to "perform" in different situations for a range of audiences. As Interviewee, this requires you to show excellent skills in all aspects of both the job description and the interview process.

Get the Teaching Job YOU Want is different from other job interview guides that you might have come across because it uses Neuro-Linguistic Programming and hypnosis techniques to support you to deal with any limiting beliefs or feelings that you may have, that could [if you don't read on] become detrimental to your interview performance. As you know, schools/academies are now run as businesses, so it's not surprising that over recent years, teaching has become more and more competitive. Hence, the interview process has become more rigorous. At the end of the day, teachers in the classroom are unique from any other professionals in as much as they are holding the future in their hands. The children/students in your class will be the workers, key workers and leaders of the future, pending your ability to inspire your learners to achieve their best, so that they can inspire the world.

By reading this text and completing the exercises within, you'll develop an understanding of the key skills and attributes that separate those candidates who secure a job quickly and those that get stuck on the interview circuit. Neuro-linguistic Programming [NLP] and Hypnosis techniques are used so that you can train your brain not only to be in the right emotional state to secure your teaching job, but also to introduce you to a range of skills that have the potential to transform your life as a teacher and beyond. I say that because after 17 years in school leadership and having gained the Licensed Practitioner of NLP, I went back to the classroom for 3.5 years, to realise the difference that this new skill set would make. I can honestly say that teaching had never been easier because I had the skills always to be emotionally ready for the task in hand. And, the skills to lead my [class] audience to be emotionally confident to learn well. In the chapters that follow, I use the same skills to support you to do this for yourself in the first instance.

The NLP techniques included in this workbook are all based on the skills that I learnt from being a novice NLPer to becoming an NLP trainer via The Society of NLP. The exercises included for you are all adapted from demonstrations on the numerous courses that I've been privileged to attend, as well as my own learning via personal development publications by Dr. Richard Bander [Co-creator of NLP], John La Valle [President of the Society of NLP] and publications by two of their master trainers: Tina Taylor, Co-Founder and Course Leader at the International College of Clinical Hypnotherapy and Kalliope Barlis [author of *Phobia Relief & Play Golf Better Faster*].

Whilst Ergophobia [fear of securing and maintaining a job] is rare, in my experience as an employer, most people experience some degree of performance anxiety at some point during the interview process. Glossophobia [fear of public speaking] is believed to affect 75% of the population. NLP and Hypnosis will help you to manage any unwanted feelings so that you can be confident to manage the interview process.

So, what is NLP and Hypnosis and how will they help in the context of getting the job you want?

Worksheets Download

If you'd prefer not to write in this book, worksheets for all exercises are available by scanning the QR code below:

Neuro Linguistic Programming [NLP]

Neuro Linguistic Programming [NLP] is a set of techniques used, primarily, as an approach to personal development. NLP studies the structure of how humans think and experience their world and provides a powerful tool that is effective in changing human behaviour and capacities.

Dr Richard Bandler coined the term "Neuro-Linguistic Programming" in the 1970s. He was recently asked to write the definition that appears in the Oxford English Dictionary. It says: Neuro-Linguistic Programming is...

"...a model of interpersonal communication chiefly concerned with the relationship between successful patterns of behaviour and the subjective experiences (esp. patterns of thought) underlying them...a system of alternative therapy based on this which seeks to educate people in self-awareness and effective communication, and to change their patterns of mental and emotional behaviour."

In the context of supporting you to, *Get the Teaching Job YOU want*, NLP techniques and language patterns are used to programme your mind, similar to programming a computer, so that your thought processes underpin success. Richard Bander notes, for example, that remembering what you can't do leads to hesitation; whereas, thinking about what you want to do and making big, bright pictures in your mind of yourself succeeding leads to motivation.

This workbook gives you a precise plan and the skills you need to be motivated to get your job application and interview preparation done and enjoy the journey along the way. Interview candidates that have been coached by me and have enjoyed the interview process much more than they ever thought possible, have thanked me profusely and often noted, "These are the skills we should learn in college", and I couldn't agree more. So, in the absence of having college tutors or equivalent trainers with the skills required via an education, recruitment & NLP/Hypnosis background, this text is my solution for you to support yourself to ensure that your learning to date continues to impact each and every step of your career ladder.

What is Hypnotherapy?

Hypnosis describes a relaxed state that you are already aware of. It may be through mediation, prayer, imagination, daydreaming, guided imagery or relaxation. It enables you to take your attention from the world outside of your mind, to a focused place within.

Hypnotherapists like me, are trained to guide you into that focused state or "trance" to support you to overcome current difficulties and achieve your goals more easily. In this state, the mind becomes particularly receptive to suggestion and is somehow able to exert control over behaviours that are normally involuntary. So, while you are in trance, a hypnotherapist can make suggestions to your sub-conscious mind to support you to achieve your goals; in this case, getting the teaching job [or promotion] you want.

Hypnosis [trance] successfully aids personal development because it is a process by which clients can see themselves having completed the change they wish to make. This works because the unconscious doesn't know the difference between real life and make believe. The hypnosis download that accompanies this book,

"A Trance to Shine at Interview", is designed to support you to rehearse thoroughly and achieve your best interview performance yet.

Thank you for trusting your instinct and purchasing this book; now trust again, read on and know that by training your brain to direct it to where you want it to go, you're on the right track to secure that teaching job that you desire most. Enjoy the journey...

Warmest wishes
Tanya

Hypnosis Download

If you would like to purchase the hypnosis download that complements this book:

YOUR TRANCE TO SHINE & GET THE TEACHING JOB YOU WANT

please visit Tanya's website at:

www.tanyabuntingcoaching.org

1

You and Your Dream School

Who are you and what do you want?

"If you can dream it, you can do it."
WALT DISNEY

As you start to read this book, my best guess is that you're a busy teacher-training student about to apply for your first job, or an even busier established teacher considering the prospect of a new school or promotion. Either way, the prospect of researching a teaching post, applying for the job and giving your best at interview can be a daunting prospect. Maybe, you've been putting it off for one reason or another and you just need the right inspiration and support to get the process off to a flying start. If that sounds like you, please be assured that most of us, however successful, have been there feeling the pressure of finding a job and willing ourselves to find whatever it takes to get on with it.

As a personal development and career coach, I often find that it's not until clients articulate what they want and what it's going to do for them, that they can start the process of transformation or in this context, the interview process. By the end of this chapter, you'll have visualised your dream school/job and be able to say what it is about you and your core purpose that resonates with the vision and values of your envisaged school. You'll have a good idea of what you're looking for, what you can offer them and vice versa. Your brain doesn't know the difference between real life and make believe, so working with your imagination is a good primer in preparation for researching the job market and starting the interview process.

Whether you're an NQT or an experienced teacher, the key steps to be the winning candidate are the same. Imagine how good you'll feel when you've combined your learnings from this book with your good resources and secured the teaching job you want. Enjoy the journey...

Years ago, I got back to my Mum's after viewing a local first school in a very middle-class area that was advertising for a Deputy Headteacher.

"What was it like?" my Mum enquired as I walked into the kitchen.

"It was okay," I replied, "but I got the distinct feeling that the headteacher had no interest in me!"

"She has no idea who you are," my mother replied, "and it's definitely not the school for you!"

"You don't know that," I retorted sitting down at the kitchen table, "I quite liked the school and it's got a great reputation."

"A great reputation alone, doesn't make it right for you," my Mum insisted, handing me some tea and sitting down for a chat.

I sipped my tea and pondered, unable to think what I could have possibly said or done to cause such disinterest. Maybe, she's heard that I was on maternity leave or maybe she'd heard something...on the grapevine! As for my mum, she left school when she was fifteen and she wasn't a teacher, so how could she possibly know which school was right for me?

"What's happening with the current Deputy?" my Mum enquired.

"She's got a Headship," I answered feeling quite disheartened. "A shock for the school, I guess. She's been there years!"

"Where's she going?" my Mum asked curiously.

Before I could even finish saying the school name, my Mum [now a complete KNOW All!] uttered, "Go with her, that's the school for you."

Hearing my little poppet stirring in her cot, I left the room noting curtly, "They already have a deputy and that post may never come up."

"Mark my words," she called up the stairs, "I can see you there...It's d-e-f-i-n-i-t-e-l-y the job for you!"

A few months later, having finished [or so I thought] the second day of interviews at "said" school, I was sitting with another candidate awaiting the outcome. The Chair of Governors popped out from the interview room to say, "It's not over yet! At the moment, we're not sure and we've got one more question to ask you both..."

The other candidate who had been invited through to the final afternoon was invited in first, so I pretty was sure the job was hers. In seconds, she was out, and I was in.

"This estate's got one road in," noted a governor, "...and it's the same road out! How are you going to win the hearts of the locals?" *

My simple answer was the WINNING reply! I had grown up spending time with one of the extended families. I knew what the locals were about and would do my best for their children.

"You were right," I sobbed, a few years later, when at the end of a long day of celebrations my dear Mum helped me pack up my classroom and leave for my first headship. And needless to say, the tears flowed even more when the locals were at the end of the school drive to cheer me off!

Driving home, I asked my Mum to reiterate how she'd known it was the job for me.

"I just knew that you'd have a heart for the families and love it," and you know what, she was right!

Thinking back to my first visit, the traditional "tour", the school in question felt right from the start and those first impressions are still clear in my mind...an inspiring and honest headteacher whose vision and values matched my own, little people with big personalities that made me laugh from the onset and an environment that promised the best journey for me. After my visit, I left the school full of excitement and wrote my application without coming up for air! It was a doddle because I could see myself there.

Politically correct comment for, "This is the roughest estate in the area, how will you relate to our community?"

In Neuro-Linguistic Programming [NLP], we talk about **Logical Levels**. This model, created by Robert Dilts, illustrates clearly the important point my Mum was trying to make back in her kitchen, all those years ago.

In NLP, the word "Congruence" describes the sense of ease and purpose that we all feel when something feels right. This can be a job, a relationship, a solution or something else, and to be truly congruent it has to be right on all levels, as shown in the illustration on the next page.

When working with my coaching clients, they sometimes discover that they've been paying attention to some areas in their lives to the detriment of others. When they realise what it is that is incongruent, they know where to put their efforts to make the difference. Needless to say, that when something feels right on all levels it's apparent in the way that you feel and results in how much more you can achieve.

Thinking back, I recall that in my letter for Deputy Headship, I had noted that the environment has to be right for me to excel. The interview panel challenged this statement, requesting a full explanation of what I meant. At the time, I hadn't even heard of Logical Levels, but now I sit here writing this opening chapter I recall how important it was for the physical

Logical Levels

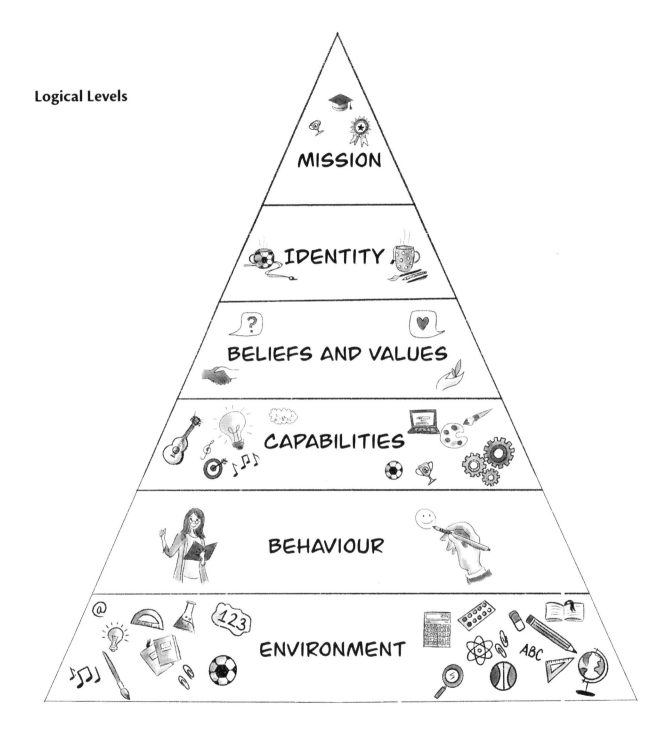

environment and relationships to be right for me to do my best. In fact, my thoughts drift back to the major disappointment of failing the 12+. At 16, still harping on about going to Grammar school, I applied for the sixth form. I hated the student interview at the Girl's Grammar School because I felt like a sore-thumb. Need I say anymore?

These days, whenever a teaching/student client tells me they've been to interview and not secured the job, I always point out that maybe…just maybe…it wasn't the job for them; and reassuringly, in my experience, they'll just know when it's right for both them and the school. That is to say, trust your instinct. When you've found the right school to work in, your gut will probably know!

Both of my headships were secured on my first application. I did my homework and followed my gut, knowing the schools for me. As time went by and lessons were learnt, the key questions to myself when considering a school position were always: Can I see myself here? Does it feel right? Can I have impact here?

To that end, and in preparation for reading adverts and deciding which schools might be right for you, I invite you to complete the following exercise. Articulating your personal response and articulating key aspects of your dream school using the Logical Levels model is designed to be twofold.

Firstly, you'll get to know your "teacher" self even better; informing the personal attributes aspect of your personal statement [more on this in Chapter 4]. Secondly, you'll create your own propulsion system, so you are motivated and inspired to get the teaching job you want!

Have fun as you get to know your logical levels in the context of you and your dream school. Before you start, take 5-10 minutes close your eyes, go inside and imagine the teaching job of your dreams. Read the instructions before you start and create your dream school using all of your senses. By closing your eyes and going inside you can focus your attention on the task in hand.

Exercise 1

Visualisation: Imagine your dream school

1. Choose a place and time when you can visualise without being disturbed.

2. Take three deep breaths in through your mouth and out through your nose. On the third breath, close your eyes, relax and go inside.

3. In your mind's eye begin to imagine your dream school. Notice how it looks, the shapes, colours, people; all the things that catch your eye. Take time to look around and realise all the things that are important to you.

4. Listen up…What sounds, words, phrases do you hear that tell you this is the right teaching job or school for you?

5. Be intuitive. Notice exactly how you feel inside when something feels right.

6. Be curious. Notice whether there are any smells or odours. Maybe there's something that creates a taste in your mouth.

7. As you look around, begin to realise what inspires and motivates you. What do you see, hear, feel that tells you it's right for you and that you can and will have impact here?

8. When you're finished, take 2-3 activating breaths to bring yourself back to a full waking state, and record your observations quickly and succinctly using the bullet points below:

My dream school…

_____
_____
_____
_____
_____
_____
_____
_____
_____
_____
_____
_____
_____
_____
_____

Tip: Some clients tell me that they can't visualise and that's okay. This exercise is designed simply to enable you to get a sense of who you are, what you want and the type of school where you can see yourself.

Exercise 2

Logical Levels: Explore your personal attributes and values in connection with your dream school/job.

Environment

Explore the link between you as a teacher and the type of school you achieve your best.

Key Question	My response	My dream school/teaching job
As a teacher, where do you operate at your best?		
Where do you feel most inspired?		
In your teaching life, where are you most content?		
Thinking colleagues, who do you work best with?		

Behaviour

Explore your actions as a teacher within your dream school environment.

Key Question	My response	My dream school/teaching job
What are you doing at school?		
What are you not doing?		
What do you need to do?		
What is the typical behaviour here?		

Capabilities

Explore the personal qualities, knowledge and skills you have to offer your dream school.

Key Question	My response	My dream school/teaching job
What specific skills and talents do you have to offer your dream school?		
How does teaching fit well with your skills set?		
How will your dream school make best use of these to raise standards?		
What capabilities do you bring that support you to stand out as a teacher?		

Beliefs & Values

Explore what's important to you & what you believe about you within this context.

Key Question	My response	My dream school/teaching job
What's important to you as a person/ teacher?		
What does your teaching job mean to you?		
What beliefs/ assumptions do you have that support your role?		
What, if anything, do you believe/assume that may hold you back?		

Identity

Explore who you are, your ambitions and where this role may take you.

Key Question	My response	My dream school/teaching job
Who are you as a teacher?		
Who will you become?		
What roles do you want to play within your dream school?		
How does your dream school fit with your sense of who you are?		

Mission/Vision

Explore your core purpose & how it supports the vision and values of your dream

Key Question	My response	My dream school/teaching job
What is your vision for you and your learners?		
How does what is happening at your dream school fit with your core purpose?		
How does your dream school relate to other areas of your life? Or the lives of others?		
How does this ideal school/job connect with what you know about YOU?		

Key Points

Remember:

★ The more you know yourself and what you want, the more easily you'll recognise your potential dream school and the job that's right for you.

★ The importance of trusting your intuition; inclination is as important as reason.

★ Taking time now to prepare yourself for the application and interview process is your personal investment in *your* future, whether you decide to self-coach or work with a professional development coach.

2

Researching Your Dream Job

Are you researching and reflecting enough to ensure it's the job for you?

"If I have a belief that I can do it, I shall surely acquire the capacity to do it even if I may not have it at the beginning."
GANDHI

The recruitment process can be exciting on the one hand and daunting on the other, for both the applicant and employer alike! I say this because I've been "privileged" to consider the job market wearing one or other "hat" on numerous occasions. As a school leader, my motive was always to compose an advert that would inspire the best teachers to want to work with us. Getting the wording right was always a responsibility and a challenge. As an applicant and potential employee, I found that a single word or phrase could invoke confidence or doubt in my mind regarding my ability to fulfil the brief and/or whether the school was right me.

I'm guessing that at this stage of the game you will have already scanned the job market. If not, you will want to get started by:

★ Talking to your network
★ Researching on social media [Facebook, LinkedIn, Twitter, Instagram]
★ Googling schools in your chosen area; visiting the vacancies section on their website and accessing the full application pack for any jobs that you are interested in
★ Visiting the "Find a Job in Teaching" area on your government's website, e.g. gov.uk, or similar

Maybe you've read a full application pack and decided to apply with little or no hesitation, or maybe you've read an application pack and doubted whether you fully meet all the criteria. If the latter is true for you, it may be reassuring to know that whilst school leaders work closely with Human Resources [HR] to attract a "field" of high-quality candidates and deter anyone else, they expect applications from candidates who are "work in progress".

The purpose of this chapter is twofold. Firstly, to support you to manage your thoughts and feelings well as you begin to work through the application process; and secondly, to support you to interpret the application pack accurately to inform your next steps.

Thinking back, I remember a rollercoaster of feelings as I worked through the application process. In one school that I worked in before the days of online advertising, the staff who were on the interview circuit would gather in the staffroom to peruse the job bulletin. As school names and positions were called out by whoever got to the booklet first, people's ears would prick up and the discussion would start. This included all sorts of speculation and mindreading, as well as questions and pokes! I can still hear it now...

"I wonder who's leaving?"

"Maybe, such and such has got a promotion?"

"Who do you think will apply?"

"Not sure I'd want to work there..."

"Tanya, this one's for you. Go and ring them now!"

And so on...

I recall one occasion when my headteacher invited me into her office because she had something to show me. There on the screen was the advert for my first headship. I immediately burst into tears because whilst I knew it was the job for me, I loved it where I was! That night, as I pondered over the advert, I rode the emotional rollercoaster lurching from excitement to self-doubt, a smidgeon of self-belief and back to excitement again.

These days, when coaching teachers or NQTs to be, I witness colleagues doing the same...

"I'm not sure, Tanya, the advert says they want an exceptional teacher; what do you think?"

Or, "They're looking for creativity and innovation; I'm not sure if my ideas will be good enough."

Or even, "What's the point? I'm not even sure I'll ever be outstanding. They clearly want someone better than me!"

When reading an advert for the first time, it's important to remember that we're all human and the nature of the beast is to doubt ourselves from time to time. However, if we think about the lottery, you have to be in it to win it! So, however you feel upon first reading of the advert, it is important to remember that self-belief is everything when applying for a job. For this reason, you should read and reread all of the information in the application pack. Typically, this will include the advert, job description, person specification, as well as key information about the school usually via the school website and the most recent OfSTED report. This process alone may be all you need to convince yourself that you have much to offer the school. As one teacher reflected when I asked about her initial feelings after reading an advert, *"Sometimes, I feel overwhelmed with the words they use but once I have read it [the advertisement] a couple of times and understood everything, I research the* *school and if possible organise a visit. If that is not possible, I ring them to see if it's possible to speak to anyone with my questions."* For this teacher, understanding the information and having any questions answered enabled her to decide if she had all the skills she needed to apply for the job.

Knowing whether a specific job is right for any of us is, of course, a very personal decision. Furthermore, the chances are that as you read and reflect on the application pack, you'll realise what it is that resonates with you and be able to decide on your next step, i.e. whether to visit the school with a view to applying. The Logical Levels exercise completed at the end of Chapter 1 will support you and the following questions are designed to probe your thinking even further.

Exercise 1
Read and reflect

As you read the advert, job description, person specification and key information about
the school consider the following questions to inform your next steps.

Logical Levels	Questions	Answers *Suggestion: Use bullet points as you complete this task quick and easily using what you know about the school, as well as your intuition. This reflection is for you. You can go into more detail when you're writing for other audiences, i.e. the selection and interview panels.*
Mission	What is the school mission/vision statement? Is this something that you can "sign" up to?	
Identity	What personal attributes is the school looking for in their desired candidate? Does the remit sound like you?	
Beliefs/ Values	What are the core values of the school? How well do these match your personal values?	
Capabilities	What knowledge and skills does the school expect of their desired candidate? How well do you match their request?	

Logical Levels	Questions	Answers
		Suggestion: Use bullet points as you complete this task quick and easily using what you know about the school, as well as your intuition. This reflection is for you. You can go into more detail when you're writing for other audiences, i.e. the selection and interview panels.
Behaviour	What does the school expect you to do? How well do you see yourself completing this role and responsibilities?	
Environment	Thinking about the physical environment as well as the school team...What have you seen or read about that attracts you to this school at this time in your teaching career? How does the school plan to support you?	
Overall	Having reviewed the application pack, can you see yourself working in this school and having impact?	

If, after reading all of the information and answering the questions above, you are really keen to apply and feel confident in your ability to be the successful candidate, you should make an appointment to visit the school [if appropriate]. Thereafter, you're advised to read Chapter 4 before your visit.

If, however, there is an aspect or aspects of the Job Description or Person Specification that cause you to doubt yourself, you are invited to complete the following exercise before scheduling your school visit.

In NLP, self-doubt is known as a limiting belief. That is to say, an assumption that may hold you back. The following exercise is designed for you to change your limiting belief by reflecting on the resources [proven skills and success] that you already have.

Exercise 2
Create and Install a Powerful Belief

Follow steps 1-3 below, then install your new belief by repeating the Visualisation exercise in Chapter 1.

Prepare to Install an Empowering Belief

	EXAMPLE	Record your belief information here...
1. My old limiting belief	I can't be new to the profession and an exceptional teacher at the same time.	
2. My new empowering beliefs	• I am a work in progress in developing my teaching skills. • Evidence shows that me and my current class are making progress over time. • I am a reflective practitioner who plans each and every lesson to be better than the last.	
3. My new and empowering belief statement	Every day, in every way, I am honing my skills to be an even more exceptional teacher.	

Key Points

Remember to:

★ Start researching the job market as soon as possible.

★ Read the full application pack, website and OfSTED report [UK only] for any jobs you are interested in, noting how well the post reflects you and what you are looking for.

★ Create, install and strengthen a powerful belief, as necessary; and consider working with a professional NLP coach if you're aware of any further doubts or limiting beliefs.

3

VIP for a Day

Are you ready to make the most out of your school visit?

To visit or not to visit, that is the question! Having read and been inspired by the full job application pack, you may be in two minds about whether to visit the school prior to submitting your application. The purpose of this chapter is to inform your decision and support you to prepare well.

In the UK, the greatest majority of primary schools and many secondary schools offer prospective candidates an informal visit and ALWAYS for senior leadership posts. As a young teacher [and lactating Mum], I didn't always make the most of this opportunity due to my perceived lack of time as well little understanding of the importance and usefulness. Years later, as a headteacher leading the recruitment process, I made school visits an important part of the recruitment and selection process. I understood that some candidates would struggle due to cost and distance, so built in opportunities for interviewees to have a "free run" of the school, during the selection process. Furthermore, I prioritised time in my diary to lead informal tours myself with a team of Year 6 children who not only applied for their "jobs" but were also trained to lead the process. This gave me the opportunity to know the context of each and every candidate's tour and to review our learning environment through fresh eyes – mine as a and the candidates! And, for me, there's a magical moment to be had when you meet a young person or step into a classroom for the first time...I wanted to know which potential teachers would see, hear, feel and share the magic...

Over the years, I have toured many schools in

all sorts of guises…prospective student, teacher, parent; as well as headteacher, Key Stage 1 SATs Moderator, visiting headteacher and/ or consultant…To name but a few! The tours that stand out in my mind do so for all sorts of reasons. For the purpose of this chapter, I'll recall just a few to inform your own thoughts about your pre-visit, the preparations and what to you plan to see, hear and feel for.

To say that all schools are not the same, is an understatement. However, the ethos be it good, bad or indifferent, is always apparent in seconds and we're all free to draw our own conclusions; apart from inspectors, of course, who are working to an agreed criterion.

Our son was eager and ready for school by the time he was three, which prompted us to look at a range of providers. I recall one school where every four-year-old was sitting in silence and copywriting and another where there was a vast range of free flow activities in a self-service environment. In one setting, the adults were savouring every ounce of effort and talking about each success; one celebration followed the next. In the other, everyone got on independently for the time that I was there. The atmosphere in each is still tangible now as I look back over 25 years!

Applying for deputy headships meant that I was also met and shown around by the headteacher on a number of occasions. That seven second window when we, as humans, suss each other out is still clear in my mind. In one school, the "best" is an aspiringly middle-class area, I remember how uncomfortable we both felt on meeting each other…it didn't bode well! I felt like I'd disturbed the headteacher's day and zoomed around so quickly that it felt like we were on roller skates! Two further visits stand out in my mind because I didn't even have to announce myself; both headteachers in their prospective schools opened the front door, knew who I was, thanked me for coming and genuinely enjoyed sharing their schools. The first had led the same school for a decade and allowed me to set the pace, only moving us through the school when I'd really seen, heard and felt what was happening. I talked…a lot! And she listened intently, genuinely interested in the things that I noticed. No questions asked. The other had recently taken up her post and shared the school vision with passion; her love for the community was tangible and she took time to show me what I needed to see…huge potential to have significant impact. A few weeks later, when I toured the same school again with a parent governor as part of the interview process, a little boy in Year 1 wolf whistled at me really loudly! He had perfected a wolf whistle that sounded more like a

30-year-old builder, than a 6-year-old at school. Needless to say, the moment was priceless, and the attention was all on me. More about my response later...

As a Key Stage 1 SATs moderator, I got to visit 10-12 schools annually. One of the four-form entry schools stands out clearly in my mind because of its exquisite visuals – giant sized paintings and huge sculptures decked the halls, handwriting in almost every Year 2 book was stunningly cursive, and the perfect presentation was mirrored in the way that every adult and young person wore their school "uniform", Needless to say, I wasn't surprised when the headteacher noted "Pride" being their key core value. Years later, I visited the same headteacher in another school in another county as part of my role on the SCITT Management Board. On this occasion, not only do I recall more amazing visuals, but an adaptable learning environment for a wealth of interventions. Imagine if Centre Parcs designed learning environments and you can picture it now! Other clear memories in my moderator role include a cosy country school with a learning loft where the kettle was on; I was served coffee and then invited to keep helping myself! And, a school at the opposite end of the friendliness scale where I was greeted by a curt voice saying, "You're not in the diary and the head's not here!"

Most recently, I visited a school where consistency was evident on every wall in every classroom, so much so that when I commented, a teacher replied, "It always looks the same at this time of year!" And so, the bubble was burst!

As a prospective candidate, you will want to notice what's important to you [Your Logical Levels] and what's important to the school ethos [Vision, Values, Principles, Policies & Policies into Practice]. You may even see, hear or feel more than you bargained for like my wolf whistle or the day when a parent exclaimed with a "Phwoah" that, "...head teachers didn't look like that [me] in my day"! Whatever you witness or experience, the important thing for you is to notice EVERYTHING that will support YOU to respond appropriately so that you:

1. **Make a good first impression** – ALL eyes, ears and instincts will be on you from the onset. The Leadership Team will be considering their next investment and the whole community will be getting, "Curiouser and curiouser," as Alice in Wonderland would say.

2. **Decide whether it's the school for you**. If you can see yourself working there, it most probably is.

3. **Write a WINNING application** that shows what impact you can have on the future success of the school.

4. **Know the context well** to inform YOUR best interview presentation yet! Notice what the school is already doing well, how it can improve further and the specific contribution you can make.

Imagine, how much more easily you can personalise a personal statement and write a winning application when you have all the information that you need to align the vision of the school with what you personally have to offer. So, in preparing for that all-important visit, do think as much about what you want to show the school, albeit informally, as much as you want to glean from them. As I said before, ALL eyes, ears and instincts will be on you and whilst I'm not going to tell you to take time to plan your "entrance", you may be curious to read on to inform how well you decide to present yourself.

Most schools will ask you to make an appointment via a telephone call to the school office. The receptionist may have access to the "tour guides" diary or may put you through to speak to the relevant person directly. My practice was to block out times for what was fondly known behind the scenes as "Tan's TOURS," on my school calendar, so that whoever answered the phone could make the appointment straight away. Thereafter, I could access the list of candidates on my calendar to know who to expect. Some members of staff would simply make the appointment, and others would take responsibility for being my eyes, ears and instinct! I recall many occasions when a certain PA, who wore her heart on her sleeve, would "advise" me about the candidate noting, things like, "I've just taken a phone call from a delightful NQT who was really understanding when I explained that you can only show her around on Thursday, this week," or "You might want to look out for this one who was really demanding when I said that you might not be able to make HIS preferred time; and he didn't do himself any favours when he said he didn't want to visit us tomorrow because he's waiting to hear back from an Outstanding school!"

Leading "Tan's Tours" was always exciting for me as a school leader and different groups and individual candidates still stand out in my mind for all sorts of reasons; not least the seven second window...

Group tours were scheduled as necessary and each visitor contributed to the dynamic. Generally, the Year 6 students would guide one visitor each, which freed me up to spend some time with each candidate. We always met people at the door and started in my office or the school hall, so that people could hear from me the headlines about our school and the context for the tour. I remember one tour where I greeted each person as he or she arrived and the "tour guide" did the same. Some candidates greeted both me and the child with a smile and shared their name whilst others took our hands but were unsure from the onset. Conversely, I recall one lady dominating a group and interviewing me about all sorts of information that was readily available online and had no idea about the irritation she was causing. Two others chatted freely to each other, completely ignoring their invaluable tour guides; whilst others interacted freely and cherished hearing about the school from the children's perspective. The displays exemplified our core purpose well and the children confidently answered any questions asked. And of course, you'll know which prospective candidates still had endless questions at the end of the tour!

Candidates that I showed around on an individual basis were on occasions over confident and felt like hard work, whilst others were understandably a bit nervous and welcomed a sensitive approach.

One of my most enjoyable tours was with Katie, a prospective early year's teacher whom I welcomed at the front door. She smiled, shook my hand, told me her name and that she'd heard a lot about the school and couldn't wait to look around. We started the tour in my office where she sat down at my invitation. She was well presented and maintained good eye contact as I shared key information about our vision and values and she briefly told me about her current plans. As we toured the school, she was visibly at ease in our setting, beamed each time she saw a new group of children and paid close attention as we visited each and every learning environment. She asked poignant questions about the role and responsibilities. At the end, she thanked me for my time and expressed how much she'd enjoyed her visit, requesting an application pack and noting her excitement about writing the application. And, I believed her because what she expressed was congruent with what I'd witness throughout the tour. Katie's attention to detail proved to be second to none when she hand-delivered her application form the next day along with a thank you card addressed to me personally.

The following exercises are designed for you to manage your feelings in preparation for your school visit. Even the most confident people can experience "butterflies" from time to time so it's a good idea to pre-empt it, don't you think? The 7-11 breathing technique is widely used to counteract anxiety by using the Parasympathetic Nervous System; the opposite of the Sympathetic Nervous System that triggers the fight, flight, freeze response. I first learnt this technique from Tina Taylor, NLP Master Trainer and author of her book *Painless Childbirth*. Using breathing to calm the neurology is well-known in many cultures and is integral to the practice of Meditation or Mindfulness, and it's something that you're already used to doing on a daily basis; for example, as you settle down to sleep at night.

Richard Bandler, Co-creator of NLP always tells his students, "If you change how you think, you change how you feel and if you change how you feel you change what you can do." The NLP Spinning Feelings exercise starts with a thought and enables you to feel how you want to feel in seconds. NLP Anchoring enables you to save a good feeling, so that you can re-access it whenever you need it. Enjoy...

Exercise 1
Keep Calm and Breathe!

1. Breathe in for a count of 7...

2. Breathe out for a count of 11...

3. Repeat this pattern for a few minutes, noticing that increasing sense of CALM as you complete each round...

Exercise 2
NLP Spinning Feelings and Anchoring

Step 1: Dissolving Discomfort

1. Think of something that puts you out of your comfort zone; remember what you see, hear, feel when you're uncomfortable or nervous [e.g. Meeting someone new, public speaking, walking into an interview].

2. Notice the feeling inside your body. Where does it start? How does it move? Which direction does it spin? [Clockwise? Anti-clockwise? Forwards? Backwards?] Top-tip: To realise this easily, move your hand in the four directions and sense which direction "fits" best with what you're feeling inside.

4. Slow the feeling down. Notice how you can make it STOP!

5. Now, spin it in the opposite direction and notice that discomfort dissolve.

Step 2: Increasing Confidence

1. Think of something you do with confidence; remember what you see, hear, feel when you're confident.

2. Notice which direction the confident feeling spins [Clockwise? Anti-clockwise? Forwards? Backwards?]

3. Focus your mind to **speed up** that confident feeling…make it go faster in the same direction; double the feeling.

4. As you sense that growing feeling of confidence, **anchor it** by squeezing your thumb and middle finger together.

5. Break your emotional state by answering a question like: What did you have for breakfast?

6. **Test your anchor:** Squeeze your thumb and middle finger together and feel confident all over again.

7. Now, remember to fire off that Confident Anchor whenever you need it [e.g. when meeting key staff at your potential dream school]

Key Points

Remember to:

★ Rehearse your introduction and make the most of that seven second window to impress your prospective employee – a genuine smile, comfortable handshake, maintained eye contact, clear speaking voice and appropriately smart appearance make all the difference. [Use: Visualisation Strategy, Chapter 1]

★ State your name as you shake hands and note how pleased you are to meet your tour guide; a handshake suggests compliance or otherwise, so aim to get it right.

★ Plan in advance to ask questions that are relevant to you and the post you're applying for.

★ Be curious: Listen with all of your senses, making a mental note of anything that will support your application.

★ Ask yourself the following questions before, during and after your school visit: Can I see myself here? What impact can I secure for this school community?

4

Writing a Winning Application

How to be top of the leader board
& secure your interview!

I wonder whether you've ever picked up a book that you couldn't put down? Or, given up on the opening chapter because you know it's not for you? How is it that some authors are instantly successful, and others fail miserably? As far as job applications go, I very nearly learnt the hard way!

Back in 1991, I was nearing the end of my first year of teaching and had no idea if my contract would be renewed. We had a temporary Headteacher at the time who announced she was leaving to take up a substantial headship at a BRAND-NEW SCHOOL! I didn't realise the implications until the Deputy Headteacher also announced her resignation and declared her excitement because she too was leaving to join the BRAND-NEW SCHOOL! I couldn't help myself, I had to find out more...

A few days after they received my application for class teacher, the Deputy Headteacher "kindly" popped in to my classroom to say that I wasn't getting an interview on account of my letter. "Your application's just not good enough," she announced, about turned and was gone. Gutted, I drove home, ruminating all the way! And resolving never to put myself through that torment again. Enough was enough!

Twenty or so years later, I sat in my conservatory on a hot, sunny day wading through applications during a work at home day. I was swamped by 128 class teacher applications for a grand total of just four jobs. A kind administration assistant had already sorted them into alphabetical order and prepared a shortlisting grid, so all I had to do was read and score them "by the book", or so I tried to tell myself.

Early in my Deputy Headship, I was privileged to attend a well-presented recruitment day. The head of Human Resources presented a fool-proof system for advertising and recruiting within the realms of the law. Equal opportunities were at the heart of the matter and, by the end of it, I knew how to write an advert, job description and person specification; as well as how to use them to avoid being sued! I sat in the audience realising that stories about applications going straight in the bin might not be strictly true and years later when two applicants questioned our practice, I was "delighted" to pass endless hours of reading and scoring over to the head of HR for her scrutiny and feedback to the relevant unions and employment tribunals.

The good news is that not only did the recruitment course help me to keep my nose clean, it also prepared me to write **winning** personal statements for my subsequent applications for headship; not to mention the "Job Coaching" support for colleagues and clients that eventually followed.

In NLP, we talk about Chunking. You chunk up to see the big picture and chunk down to spot the detail. In essence, a Job Description [JD] and Person Specification [PS] provide the smaller chunks. In a nutshell, best practice requires that each applicant is scored alongside each criterion on the PS, with the JD in mind. It therefore doesn't take a genius to realise that if you reverse the process and write your letter of application in the order of the documents, making sure that you "tick every box", you'll be well on the way to a winning application. There is another "magic" ingredient that I will share with you, but not just yet!

First of all, I want to go back to my conservatory on that hot, sunny day when I very nearly lost the plot. Scoring every application alongside 25 or more criteria is never easy, at the best of times. BUT, having initially been over the moon that so many applicants wanted to work at our school, the sheer volume of applications was onerous, to say the least. Furthermore, the greatest majority of applicants had little structure to their applications so scoring them was a bit like looking for needles in a haystack. And that's before I even comment on the quality or expression. Thereafter, the letters that followed the structure of the Person Specification fell into three categories:

1. Most or all criteria mentioned; paraphrased only.

2. Most or all criteria mentioned and personalised by the candidate with reference to what they could bring to the school.

3. As 2, with the extra "magic" ingredient!

To my relief, within the piles, there were plenty of well written, unique and lively statements that invoked great excitement. These, I seemed to read at speed and could score them easily; as opposed to the ones that I had to force myself to read to keep going. If their letter was boring, whatever would it be like to be a student in their class?

You may well be thinking, "The pot's calling the kettle black," and you'd be right! As that NQT back then, I had no idea how to write a personal statement, yet alone one that would secure an interview. As luck would have it, the recipient of my application was frequently in and out of my classroom. She knew what she wanted in her BRAND-NEW SCHOOL and convinced the governors to extend the deadline so that I could update my application to something that was at least half-decent. I had 24 hours! When I got home, I settled my baby boy to bed and rewrote my application. At that point, I hadn't yet learnt the "winning" strategy of writing to the Person Specific. Nevertheless, with a more detailed application in place, I secured an interview and a new job; albeit against the odds!

Today, I'm still amazed that so many students leave our schools and universities still lacking the knowledge of how to write a winning application. Luckily, as a reader of this text and possibly one of my students/clients, it doesn't have to be like that for you. In just a few more pages, so long as you're planning and teaching well, you'll be fully equipped to write your winning application.

Thereafter, as and when you get your "Call to interview" please remember to confirm your attendance. As a busy headteacher of a large school, one of my pet hates was deploying staff to chase candidates who had forgotten their Ps and Qs!

So, how do you ensure a winning application and secure your interview?

How to write a winning application

1. **Be prepared!** Read and reread the Job Description and Person Specification, in light of what you already know about the values, ethos and effectiveness of the school via your research [Chapter 2]

2. **Grab the reader!** Write an opening paragraph that states exactly why you want to apply for this school at this time. The reader needs to hear your enthusiasm for their school, as well as your passion for teaching. To entice them to read on with interest, your core values and beliefs must be loud and clear.

3. **Organise your thinking!** Write your statement in the same order as the Person Specification, using the same subheadings to mirror the structure. This supports the reader to actively read, digest and score your application easily. This "mirroring" creates a clear structure for you to show precisely how well you meet their criteria. To ensure your maximum score, you must state how you meet each criterion. It's important to know that recruitment panels following best practice guidelines score each aspect separately; and, your total score determines your ranking on the "Call to interview" list.

4. **Mind your language!** Use a positive and convincing tone. Reflect key words and phrases. This builds rapport and subliminally persuades the reader to know that you "speak the same language".

5. **Be convincing!** Read and reflect on every section, then state:

   I. Precisely how you meet each criterion; don't just "go on" about how important it is!

   II. Include anecdotal evidence that enables the reader to imagine your lessons. You can do this by referring to a good lesson that you have taught recently.

   III. Convince your reader by including an *impact statement within every paragraph.

   *Magic ingredient: When you include an *impact statement* showing the impact of your teaching on your student's learning, you convince your audience of two things. Firstly, your understanding about the core purpose of their school, i.e. LEARNING. And secondly, your effectiveness at a teacher. Your audience will see you as credible when you speak from experience.

6. **Quote your data!** As with advertising, using statistical or numerical data is a great convincer. Example, *"As a result, **80% of students are on track** to meet or exceed age related targets by the end of the year."* Or, *"Consequently, **100% of students** show good attitudes to learning throughout the greatest part of every lesson."*

7. **Future Pace the Reader!** Use phrases that enable the read to imagine your impact within their school. E.g. *"I welcome the opportunity to be involved in the development of the Drama curriculum, department and*

*school life as a whole. **I also look forward** to inspiring young creatives in a variety of extra-curricular activities."*

8. **Whet their appetite!** Use the final paragraph to summarise your personal statement and then build anticipation towards your interview. E.g. *"In conclusion, I think I would work well as a member of your school community because I love my subject and I am passionate about young people and their role in a fast-developing world. I want to be part of the positivity, and shared values of [School name] to give our learners their best chance. All young people deserve to know that their teacher cares. I look forward to sharing my skills and passion for learning during the interview process."*

Exercise 1

Remember the key aspects of a lesson that went well

This activity will support you to answer/speak from experience, in order to provide anecdotal/statistical evidence. It works best if you read the instructions first and then follow them with your eyes closed. This activity will stand you in good stead for the formal interview when it's likely that you'll be required to recall a successful lesson or even one to the contrary!

1. Take a deep breath in through your nose, close your eyes and breath out through your mouth as you go inside and relax.

2. Imagine a screen on the wall in front of you, as if you were at the cinema.

3. Think back to a recent lesson that went well. Allow the memory to rerun as a "movie" in your mind. Play it from beginning to end a number of times, watching it from different viewpoints:
   I. The teacher: Step into the movie: See what you saw, hear what you heard and feel what you felt as you relive that good lesson all over again.
   II. The learners: Step into the shoes of the students and see what they saw, heard, felt...
   III. An observer: Step into the shoes of an observer and see through their eyes, hear through their ears and feel how they felt...

4. Reflect on the impact of teaching on learning: Each time you watch, notice what you say/do and how the children respond. Open your eyes and record any notes, as appropriate. Tip: Wait until the end of the memory movie, so that your experience flows, and you remember the factors that made the biggest difference.

Key Points

Remember to:

★ Sell yourself- It's all about you and the students you'll teach!

★ Use positive or persuasive language throughout.

★ Convince your audience using anecdotal/statistical evidence; comment honestly on every section and remember points mean prizes!

★ First impressions count! Be sure to edit your spelling and grammar thoroughly or ask a friend/coach to do this for you.

Received a "Call to interview"?

★ Be sure to accept by phone and in writing. A quick call to the headteacher's secretary and following this up with an email will show your good manners and save the school a lot of hassle!

5

Prepare your References

Are you asking the right referees in the best way?

"The referee is going to be the most important person in the ring tonight, apart from the fighters."

-GEORGE FOREMAN

An employer is under no obligation to obtain a reference for a potential new employee, but it is common to seek at least one reference [usually two] and to make any job offer conditional on a satisfactory reference. Schools usually state that your teacher training tutor is the first referee for Newly Qualified Teachers [NQTs] and your current headteacher for experience teachers. Writing a high-quality reference takes time, even when pro-forma is provided. By the end of this chapter, you'll be able to appreciate the purpose and process from different viewpoints and be

well informed to decide who and how to ask.

As a headteacher, I often joked about getting the "best" jobs and some of these required perfect precision and skill. One such job was apple bobbing…

One sunny lunchtime, I was on the playground when two little Year One boys summoned me inside, insisting it was urgent. I responded immediately not least because one was walking with his legs tightly crossed and the other was insisting, "You won't believe it!" Having issued the normal warning, I waltzed into the Year 3 urinals [for the first time] realizing a moment too late that my leather soles would never be the same again. I was on the verge of chuckling when I first saw the apple bobbing in the drain, because I had, if honest, prepared myself for a far worse "treat" when suddenly the public lavatory stench hit my nose and I reversed back from the overflow that was slowly but surely leaking soiled water across the floor. Having sent for rubber gloves and positioned myself to wait on guard, you can imagine the shock I got when the old, automatic flush, roared up and a foul smelling "Niagara" came crashing down. To this day, I have no idea why the flushing system towered above me, let alone the children, unless it was designed to be the adult men's loo back in the day? Thereafter, precise skill and timing were paramount when I surreptitiously tiptoed forward, hitched up my skirt and went down on my haunches to manually retrieve the apple between flushes…If I got my timing wrong, the worst was definitely about to happen!

Back in my office, I stood at my desk having a quick dash through the post whilst the teachers called the registers. If I focused, the 5-10 minutes before assembly were just about long enough to sort the actions into urgent, asap and pending. First up was a request for a reference for a teaching assistant whom I'd line managed as a deputy head. It was needed for an interview the following day. The thought that I'd hoped not to take work home that night passed briefly through my mind and besides it would be a joy to write, she was an asset to the school after all.

A few years later, having moved onto my second headship, I returned to my office after lunch again and picked up the phone. The call was from another local head that I didn't know very well, asking for the heads up on a Mrs Such and Such because she'd applied for a teaching job and put me down as a referee and the head teacher was sorry to put me on the spot but she also wondered if I could release the lady for interview the next day. It was short notice, but they were desperate to cover a maternity leave and needed to allow time for candidates to give notice before half-term so that they could start after Easter. I sat listening with my chin on the floor before I politely replied that it was a bit of a shock…It would, of course, have been nice to know in advance and even better if she'd had the decency to ask me would I provide a reference…how rude!

On another occasion, I was contacted by HR and requested to provide the supporting evidence for a reference I had provided that didn't match the candidate's self-assessment shared during the application and interview process. I sent copies of everything that substantiated my comments and the conclusion was that I had been fair and transparent. This meant that I wasn't facing an employment tribunal and more importantly the person in question didn't find herself trying to fulfil a job where she would clearly have been out of her depth.

In terms of getting the best jobs, I actually enjoy the process of writing and most often enjoyed the art of writing a reference especially when there was much to celebrate. Like so many other headteachers I know, I would take great care to evidence particular strengths, potential and key areas for development; always noting anecdotal and statistical evidence to exemplify impact. Potential and areas for development can both be considered positive because it gives school leadership teams the opportunity to reflect on what their school can offer you and your potential to contribute even more, over time. Needless to say, that headteachers looking to employ NQTs love to grow their own! When writing both professional and personal references, I endeavour to answer the questions asked [usually about knowledge, skills and attributes] as well as drawing attention to personal values or how well the employer upheld our school values. By that, I mean things like independence, teamwork, creativity, problem solving, perseverance, open mindedness and loyalty [to the core purpose] because for me it's a person's ability to share the school or organisations vision that makes the biggest difference. Many personal values are apparent when candidates requesting a reference:

1. Contact in person, giving details about the post. This enables your referee to begin to reflect on what they know about you and be prepared when they receive a phone call or written request.

2. Briefly tell your referee about the specific impact that you feel you can make in the school that you're applying to. If you talk about transferring your skills that the referee has personally witnessed, s/he may well decide to include them.

Over the years, there have been many colleagues for whom I have been privileged to write a reference. The action of doing so has stirred my own emotions for a variety of reasons, not least the pride in acknowledging their impact on the community that we served. Most employers will summarise a reference noting something like, "I [highly] recommend [name] for the position of class teacher, without [with a few] reservations." Thereafter, they may summarise why or even go the extra mile...

Occasionally, particularly when I had time on my side, I too would go the "extra mile". The specific reference that comes to mind was for a certain middle leader who had been promoted within our community and made significant impact. So much so, that I was able to provide substantial data to exemplify the impact of her leadership on progress and suggest to the interview panel, "Please don't miss this excellent opportunity for your school community". I also asked them to, "...be aware that she's so much better than she thinks she is." A few weeks later, I was sent a message from the headteacher thanking me for a reference that was "spot on"!

When I was wearing my headteacher hat, it was particularly helpful when candidates completed all of the requested information in the references section. It wasn't unusual for candidates to leave gaps which could slow the process down if the information given didn't support our chosen route for gathering information. Whilst it's understandable that you may not carry the contact details for everyone you know, I'm sure you wouldn't want to raise doubt in a potential employer's mind about your attention to detail by failing to follow instructions and provide what they've asked for. And of course, you'll want to ensure that all referees are expecting to hear from the interview panel, especially if there's even the slightest risk that they may refuse your request. I have said, "No," for the first time recently when a teacher whom I supported over 10 years ago has worked for a number of subsequent headteachers and I knew that we had lost touch and my reference would be well and truly out of date.

And finally, back to apple bobbing...if you've ever gone in face first, you'll know that it takes skill and precision, as well as perseverance to grasp the apple you want. So, make sure you choose a referee who has the precise information and skills to come across well to help you get the teaching job you want. Over the years, the greatest majority of references I received were well written and truly reflected the candidate's knowledge, skills and attributes. A few, on the other hand, were so brief that it was blatantly evident that the referee knew little about them or had little ability or motivation to reflect them well. Be aware that however well someone knows you and the quality of your work, the quality of their presentation [good, bad or indifferent] will always reflect on you. If they're enthusiastic to give up their time to write about you, you're most probably "a good apple" and on to a winner!

Key Points

Remember to:

★ **Choose your referees wisely:** Select people that not only know you and your skill set but can also evidence your progress and the impact you've made.

★ **Remember your Ps and Qs:** Make direct contact and tell them that you would really appreciate it if they can write a reference for you and have the decency to ensure that they are one of the first to know when you are offered and accept the job.

★ **Fill the application form in and provide precise information about each referee** including their name, title, phone number, email address, school/work address.

6

How to prepare for your formal interview

Expect the Unexpected & Relish the Surprise!

"Never be nervous when given the opportunity to market your skills and talent. It's the only time when people are genuinely interested in hearing you talk about yourself."

JASON VINCIK

Your formal interview is the perfect opportunity to "sell yourself" to the interview panel. After all, they will be paying your wages at the end of each month so they will want to know exactly what they're buying; and, of course, they will want to ensure the best value for their school. By the end of this chapter, you'll know the secret to inferring the interview questions you're likely to be asked and be ready for any surprises that the panel may have in store!

During my twenty-eight years in education, I was personally interviewed for a teaching or leadership post on just eight occasions; whereas my experience of designing and leading the interview process is at least ten times that figure. As the interviewee, I can recall times when I knew the process was going well and wasn't surprised when I was offered the job; and one occasion when I knew from the onset that the odds were stacked against me. I can also recall numerous occasions as a school leader when the interview process flew by, and the odd occasion when it just dragged...when I just wanted to shout, "I'm a headteacher, get me out of here!"

If I think back to my first formal interview, I can still see the panel in my mind's eye. The headteacher, a nun, was accompanied by an older lady, the chair of governors, who was very conservative in her appearance. Sister put out her hand to greet me and was a tad surprised when I nearly shook it off! The nun did all of the talking, whilst the other lady peered at me over the top of her steel rimmed glasses and made various expressions between making endless notes. The more she raised her eyebrows, the more I tried to explain myself. At the end of the interview, they asked me to wait outside which was literally agony; not least because their decision was so important but because as that young lactating mum, I was acutely aware that Stephen was needing his lunchtime feed! After what seemed like ages, the headteacher appeared through the door of her office. Her manner was business like when she spoke, stating that I had been unsuccessful not least because the parents would consider me a spring chicken!

My second interview was after lunch on the same day. On this occasion, the headteacher was accompanied by the deputy headteacher and a Year 2 teacher. Each member of the panel shook my hand and stated their names, making it easy for me to greet each of them appropriately. Each panel member wore a dress and a jacket, and I remember feeling comfortable in my chosen dress for the occasion – a navy blue, needle cord sailor dress with a pleated skirt and low navy court shoes. The panel took it in turns to speak and each wrote their own notes. As they recorded, they each nodded agreeingly. Thinking back, I now realise that it wasn't just the nun and co that had reservations about the spring chicken or young Mother Hen! After my interview, I was whisked off to the staffroom where the chair of governors had just "happened" to pop in. She was curious to know all about me, my training and my new baby and wondered how I was going to cope with a full-time job. A while later, she left, and I waited in the staffroom for eternity before being offered the post. My answers both in and out of the interview room had obviously convinced them!

The next interview I recall was held in a bleak office because the shiny new school building was work in progress. The interview panel were sitting in front of a window and I had a dull view of the Bournemouth coastline. The windows were covered with some sort of film that not only kept the sun out but changed the whole atmosphere of the building so much so that it could have felt like I was being interviewed under a black cloud. As an NLP Trainer, I now know what I did to come across as an enthusiastic and convincing practitioner, despite the gloomy atmosphere.

The formal interview for my deputy headship felt very different, not least because I had attended a course that was aimed at securing promotion and now understood how the interview panel worked. I knew, broadly, the types of questions that would be asked. Ray C., a local authority link inspector, had led the course and explained that a panel member would ask a question and that the other members of the panel would probe if they wanted more detail. The skill, he noted, was to be able to realise the issues they were looking for even if it was an open question. Looking back, I now realise that I had over prepared to the extent that I knew my answers off by heart. Whilst this didn't stop me getting the job it did show that I wasn't calibrating my audience. They found it hard to stick to time because they couldn't shut me up! Harry T., the link inspector associated with the school was very expressive in what I now realise were unconscious and conscious cues that I wished I'd noticed sooner. At one point, he took a very long, slow intake of breath through pursed lips that in retrospect could have indicated that I was going on too long. Eventually, he used the universal "wind it up" or "get on with it" gesture [rotating finger] and I finally responded. It was the end of a long two days and no doubt tiredness and interview nerves didn't help, albeit I had the answers at my fingertips.

As an interviewer, I can now see things from Harry's point of view. Interviewees whose formal interview stands out in my mind, either positively or negatively, include the following candidates whose names have been changed to ensure anonymity:

★ Sian who maintained eye contact with the Chair of Governors and ignored the rest of us.
★ Rafael whose constant sniffing got right up my nose and whose portfolio was dog-eared and smelt of fags!
★ Anabelle who kept playing with her hair band that was on and off her wrist a number of times.
★ Jade who kept telling me things I already knew about our school and evading the question.
★ Yiannis who was so laid back that I wondered if he was on the same planet
★ Michael who had learnt textbook answers for all aspects of learning and repeated answers verbatim when we tried to probe
★ And, Miranda who repeated and asked us to repeat every question, and showed little or no emotion throughout

In comparison, I also remember:

★ Sinead who was well prepared, relaxed and articulate throughout
★ Marek who exemplified each and every answer by reflecting on his practice in the classroom
★ Janice who used her beautifully presented portfolio to justify her answers
★ Hasan who shared some carefully chosen exercise books to show the impact of teaching on learning
★ Jane whose portfolio was exquisite and used throughout part of her interview to contextualise her answers

To name but a few!

As you prepare for interview, it's important to think about how you want to be received by others. One of the presuppositions of NLP states that, "The meaning of communication is in the response you get", so you can start to prepare by paying attention to yourself and others in the classroom, the staffroom, meetings and beyond. At interview, you should be mindful that studies by Albert Mehrabian, in 1971 conclude that:

★ Words (the literal meaning) account for 7% of the overall message
★ Tone of voice accounts for 38% of the overall message
★ Body Language accounts for 55% of the overall message

You can do this well when you:

1. **Dress to Impress:** For most of us, our appearance affects our behaviour, so plan what to wear. More about that in Chapter 8.

2. **Walk in confidently and maintain good body language throughout:** Employers, especially school leaders, are far more likely to employ someone who is smiley, professional and enthusiastic; as opposed to someone who is slouching, laid back or disinterested.

3. **Build and maintain rapport:** Use an appropriate handshake, remember and use people's names and maintain eye contact/ connection with your whole audience.

4. **Communicate with confidence and be yourself:** Hear the question, think about the issues it raises and speak from experience. Linking your answers to your classroom practice and the impact you have achieved will help the audience to imagine or see you at work and make you much more credible.

If you recall what you see, hear, feel when you're teaching; your audience will make the pictures you are describing, hear your enthusiasm and feel your good energy. You know and can remember now how someone else's communication can make you feel [good or bad] so it's wise to consider how you make other people feel, is it not?

5. **Calibrate your audience:** Watch how your message is being received and respond accordingly. If they are happily nodding, the chances are that they agree with you and you're on the right track. If they look confused, you can check in with them, noting something like, "I'm not sure that I've answered the question, please can you repeat [or clarify] the question". In my experience, interviewers design the questions to help them determine the best person for the role; generally, they will want to support you to succeed so that they can inform their decision.

It's also wise to expect the unexpected and relish the surprise. At the end of this chapter, you will find a generic set of formal interview questions for you to begin to prepare your own answers. Later on, you can use the Person Specification [PS] and Job Description [JD] to infer which questions you are likely to be asked in a specific school. You can do this easily, by turning each statement or group of statements into a question, just like you would if you were designing a reading comprehension. And, that's the secret to knowing how many interview panels prepare! They may word the questions differently, but any human resources officer will advise them to prepare the JD and PS upfront and use these key documents to inform the interview design, which may also include a presentation and task, as well as the traditional lesson observation; all informed by the current priorities of the individual school, of course.

Thinking surprises and if you've read this book in order, you'll recall the question that I was asked in order to secure my deputy headship: "This estate's got one road in," noted a governor, "...and it's the same road out! How are you going to win the hearts of the locals?" Well, that one I answered confidently. I knew an extended family on the estate and had grown up playing with their children, joining them at least twice per year for Bonfire Night and Boxing Day. I knew that whatever their circumstances each and every parent wanted the best for their child, I shared that vision and would do whatever it would take to ensure that each child was happy and ready to learn. The question that threw me, was the one posed by Harry T., the link inspector. He asked me what I would be doing between being offered the job and taking up my post. After I responded that I would come in to meet the staff and bring cakes, he thanked me; so, I knew my window of opportunity had closed! As I sat in the office next door, while the panel deliberated, I can remember holding myself to ransom: Why didn't I say that I would be getting to know our school priorities, so that I could support the strategic role of the school? And knowing that I would be a teaching deputy, why hadn't I mentioned getting to know my class and their individual needs! Thinking back, I had concentrated on my presentation and the more challenging questions involved in a senior leadership interview and in my haste, neglected the basics. After two long days, I got away with it but I'm sure you would want to excel, wouldn't you?

As teachers, I believe that like any presenter, it's important to know how to be the biggest energy in the room when we need to be. So, how did I remain enthusiastic when being interviewed within those bleak offices at Dorset House? I now realise that the more I imagined myself working with an inspiring new headteacher and her handpicked team in a state of the art, brand new building, the more I became animated about my own skills and what I had to offer. Richard Bandler, co-creator of NLP,

always tells his students that our brain doesn't know the difference between real life and the imagination. So, if we can picture the future going well, our brain will imagine it happening now and produce the right chemicals for us to present well. More about that in Chapter 9.

As I think back to being that young mum at interview and the questions that were asked both in and out of the room, it is of course important to note that all schools now work within the parameters of employment law, and that equal opportunity policies and clear guidance support interview panels to avoid discrimination and ensure that all candidates are given a fair opportunity. Schools ensure equality of opportunity by asking all candidates the same initial question. With that in mind, the questions below are from a Facebook post I read recently where an unsuccessful candidate's post requested advice with regard to good answers. In 2018, the Guardian noted that 1 in 83 teachers was on long term sickness, due to stress and schools are now expected to plan for teacher well-being, so it's not surprising that candidates are now being asked about this in an appropriate way. As I didn't design the questions below, I can't be sure of the answers the schools were hoping for, so I have included the challenge questions and example answers to provide you with a strategy for designing your own answers to the questions you're expecting and any surprises the school may have in store.

As you reflect on each question, be aware of the phraseology, specifically the verb tenses and the modal operators [i.e. could, should, would]. The more you speak from experience, about your teaching methods and their proven impact to date, the more credible you will be. Telling an interview panel about how you have reflected and developed your practice to secure even better progress, will also make you more convincing. If their question propels you to the future, e.g. How could you raise standards in Reading? Tell them what you have done to date, as well as how you can develop this in their setting, as well as sharing any further ideas that you may have.

When teaching Persuasion Engineering, John La Valle, President of the Society of NLP, always asks his audience: What do you sell? Inevitably, they answer cars, clothes, fashion, houses and all sorts of other commodities. Gradually, he reveals what every salesperson [and teacher] sells is a feeling. That is to say, if you can present information [or learning] so that your audience enjoy it, you're half-way there. At interview, the content [words and phrases that reflect your understanding] are as important as how you present it. The more sensory language you use, the more your audience will feel that they know what it's like to be a learner in your classroom. Thorough preparation that reflects on your role in the classroom will support your confidence and credibility. John also gives great advice for that moment when the interview panel asks, "Do you have any questions for us?" John advises his business clients to presuppose that they'll get the job and answer, "Yes, why should I work for this company [school]?" Needless to say, you'll know that it's safe to ask this question if you've remained in rapport and given a good interview up to this point. Presuming the panel are interested, it's a great opportunity for them to share what they can offer you!

Enjoy, reflecting on the questions below. The process will enable you to realise the issues being each criterion/question and gives you the opportunity to answer from experience so that your autonomy shines through because you want to stand out from the others, don't you?

Exercise 1

Work though the questions below and use the prompts to formulate your own answers.

Interview Questions noted in recent Facebook post [reprinted with the kind permission of the author]	Challenge: What issues might the school have been raising?	Challenge: What might a successful answer include? [The suggestions are to probe your own thinking; your challenge is to add to the ideas and reflect on an appropriate answer for you]
1. What is your most positive moment during your educational training? How has it shaped the professional that you are today?	• Inspiration • Educational Success • Teacher/Mentor Feedback	• A memory that inspired or impinged confidence • Impact on relationships with students • Use of positive reinforcement, no put-downs
2. What do you feel are the major changes and challenges facing schools with the new curriculum change and how can you help us address them?	• Timetabling issues • Curriculum coverage • Knowledge & skills development • Key skills & progression • English and maths across the curriculum • Planning • Candidates personal interests & curriculum strengths	• Candidates ideas for ensuring curriculum coverage, with examples; e.g. Project or values-based curriculum, or similar • English and maths across the curriculum with a clear example of how you or the school you've been working at has made this work in practice • Ideas for planning cross curricular projects • Thoughts about which subject/s you would be confident to lead now or in the future if you're an NQT

Interview Questions noted in recent Facebook post [reprinted with the kind permission of the author]	Challenge: What issues might the school have been raising?	Challenge: What might a successful answer include? [The suggestions are to probe your own thinking; your challenge is to add to the ideas and reflect on an appropriate answer for you]
3. We place a high importance on relationships and well-being. Which relationships would you look to make, how and why?	• Awareness of the school team • Teamwork • Support for each other & everyone's well-being • Awareness of everyone's roles and responsibilities, including the learners • Knowledge of who you would go to for help • Behaviours for Learning, Rights Respecting Schools Agenda, etc.	• Knowledge of who represents the school team • Personal contribution to the team • Ideas for supporting team well-being • Appropriate expectations of all members of the school team and how the candidate will support learners and colleagues to excel, e.g. A nurturing environment, PSHCE, Mindfulness, Respect, etc.
4. Assessment of pupils learning by the teaching team is important. What do you feel is effective assessment practice and what would it look like in your foundation phase classroom?	• Teacher knowledge [formative & summative assessment] • Marking and feedback • Peer assessment • The assessment cycle [success criteria, etc]	• Candidate's personal reflection and practice • Candidate's personal beliefs & philosophy, what this will look like in the EYFS, and why; giving real life examples of good practice where possible

Exercise 2

Use the Job Description and Person Specification to formulate your own questions for a mock interview/rehearsal

If you have yet to access the key documents for a specific job and you want to get ahead of the game, you can use the following questions as a starter for 10.

General Questions	Challenge: What issues is the school asking when asking this question? [Bullet point the issues as per Exercise 1]	Challenge: What will YOUR successful answer include?
1. Tell us a bit about yourself and why you've applied for this job?		
2. You've had a chance to look around our school. What has impressed you and what could we do to improve?		

General Questions	Challenge: What issues is the school asking when asking this question? [Bullet point the issues as per Exercise 1]	Challenge: What will YOUR successful answer include?
You as a teacher/professional		
3. If I came into your classroom, what would I see? How would I know that you and your class were exceeding? How would we know that you're a good role model for our children?		
4. Reflecting back on the lesson you taught today…What went well? What might the next steps be for you and the children?		
Curriculum		
5. How do you teach Phonics? Reading? Spelling? How would you ensure that these are taught across the curriculum? [N.B. If you're a secondary/specialist teacher you can edit the question to cover the key elements of your subject]		

General Questions	Challenge: What issues is the school asking when asking this question? [Bullet point the issues as per Exercise 1]	Challenge: What will YOUR successful answer include?
6. Calculation has been identified as an area for development. How would you ensure this is EYFS? KS1/2/3/4?		
Assessment		
7. How do you find out what a student has really learnt?		
8. What would you do if you realised that a student wasn't making progress at the rate you expected? Tell us about a learner who has accelerated their learning and the part you played in achieving this.		

General Questions	Challenge: What issues is the school asking when asking this question? [Bullet point the issues as per Exercise 1]	Challenge: What will YOUR successful answer include?
Behaviour		
9. What behaviours would you expect to see in a FS, KS1,2,3,4 classroom? What else might you see and how would you address this?		
10. You're in the corridor and there's an "issue" involving two children from another class. What steps would you take and why? Scenarios: What if...a fight broke out? A child used inappropriate language? Or, tell us about a time when a learner's behaviour surprised you. What you did and why?		
Health and Safety		
11. What would you do/say if a child told you something or you noticed a mark/bruise that concerned you? Or, if you heard a learner saying that they were going away?		

General Questions	Challenge: What issues is the school asking when asking this question? [Bullet point the issues as per Exercise 1]	Challenge: What will YOUR successful answer include?
12. What 3 things would you do to ensure health and safety at all times?		
Summing up		
13. Convince us why you should be the successful candidate.		
14. If you were offered the post, would you accept it?		
15. Do you have any questions that you would like to ask us?		

Key Points

Remember to:

★ **Stay alert: Listen to the question, note the issues it raises and answer from experience; noting real life situations that you have addressed is more convincing than giving a textbook answer, especially when you note the impact of your actions on the learning outcomes.**

★ **Calibrate your audience: Speak to the whole room, note their reaction and adapt as necessary.**

★ **Use Sensory Language: If you tell your audience what they will see, hear and feel when they visit your classroom; they'll be able to imagine what it may be like to be a student in your class.**

★ **Be aware that some interview panels will request a portfolio: Select carefully chosen photographs, planning, learning outcomes, marking, assessment and anything else that you consider relevant.**

★ **Ask a trusted friend or colleague to run you through a mock interview, as soon as you feel ready; or, make an appointment with an appropriately qualified coach who can support you to prepare well.**

Top Tip:
Be aware that the school's most recent Inspection Report and/or the School Improvement Plan is highly likely to inform the questions you will be asked at interview. For example, if a school is aiming to raise standards in writing, they may well ask you to describe a recent writing lesson, note progress and the difference that made the difference.

Lesson Preparation

Making the most of your classroom audition!

"It is the supreme art of the teacher to awaken joy in the creative expression and knowledge."

ALBERT EINSTEIN

★ Are you in the process of preparing for a teacher interview?

★ Maybe, you want to present your best lesson yet?

★ I wonder if you'd be interested if I said I can teach you the secret to planning that lesson for success?

As I sit down to write this chapter, I can remember many occasions when I was called to interview...the initial excitement, followed by the overwhelm of having a family to look after, a class to teach and a "101 things to prepare" for my classroom "audition" in just a few days' time.

Over recent months, I have read endless social media posts seeking help with lesson preparation, content and resources. If you're on the same secret Facebook groups as me, you'll know the posts I mean; for example:

In your lesson observation during the interview process how do you give your lessons the absolute wow factor? This is the one thing that's let me down from getting a job at my final placement school which is the dream and I'm devastated. I was told my lesson and interview were great just someone else had the wow factor. Any advice would be greatly appreciated as I'm beginning to feel like I'll never get a job. Thank you in advance.

Hi everyone, I have a teaching observation with a year 5 class on Friday. It's 20 minutes long but struggling for ideas as I've never taught above year 3, any suggestions? I can do the lesson on anything I'd like, thanks!

What usually follows is a list of endless responses… ideas, websites, books & film resources, games, ice-breakers, warm-ups, favourite counting resources and précised versions of lessons that secured interview success…To mention but a few! I often wonder how helpful it is to be completely overwhelmed with other people's ideas when it's really important that you own the classroom stage. I'm not saying that we shouldn't "magpie" the best teaching strategies, but I am saying that your ownership is key. To be convincing and successfully "nail" your interview lesson observation, you really want to own the show. Over the years, I've seen many lessons fall down because individual teachers haven't thought them through. When leading a three-form intake school, I would often see the same lesson delivered in three different ways with varying degrees of impact. I have successfully delivered plans taught by colleagues albeit it, "My Way". I also recall a certain maths observation when I had watched the observers questioning my class and thought, "The only way is up…" All because I'd felt the pressure to deliver in a certain way.

After 17 years in school leadership, I recently returned to the classroom for a three-and-a-half-year stint. My purpose was to enjoy my journey with the children and to explore the impact I could achieve with my current skillset. It was humbling to go back to class teaching because I had certainly lost touch with the "art" of the class teacher. It was also very exciting because my job had never been easier, not least because I had finally learnt what I now call the secrets of the mindful teacher. They're not rocket science and you can learn them too.

The purpose of this chapter isn't to tell you how or what to teach. It is rather to give you "food for thought" in terms of your "supreme art" and some pointers about what Einstein may have meant when he coined the phrase to "awaken joy" in your learners. But first, an insight into a few of the interview lessons I've been privileged to watch and the response they got…

We were sitting in my office, interviewing for teaching assistants. A very smiley lady arrived, and we briefed her that 6x Year 1 children would be arriving shortly to enjoy the story that she had prepared for them. She beamed and said I can't wait. After the tiniest tap on the door, we all sat back, enchanted…In a split second, our "TA to be" had our learners feeding out of her hands. Taking a deep breath in, she opened the door, thrilled to see the learners and telling them that she couldn't wait for them to arrive... she had been told what great learners they were and wondered whether anyone could help her with a problem she had to solve. Accepting their challenge, the children sat down, each receiving a character to look after and experience the story from their point of view. The floor became a stage in the round as the children and teacher brought the story alive. My deputy and I had to write at top speed to record the rapid progress. Key questions were embedded within gentle phrases: I wonder where Tiddler might be? Every response valued and each child's thinking probed to invoke or justify inferences: He could be at the dentist because...And later when asked how the experience could lead to further creativity and knowledge, the teaching assistant noted what the children had achieved and justified an appropriate next step...In summary, my deputy and I noted that our visitor had enchanted the room, got the learning bit between her teeth and not let go and shown huge potential for securing progress within our context.

Another interview lesson that stands out in my mind involved a certain Early Years Foundation Teacher whose "audition" started as she walked into our reception classroom. She wasn't phased by all 30 children jumping up to see what she'd brought them; she welcomed their enthusiasm, handed out the resources, turned up the volume and invited us all to our first dough disco. My chair of governors and I giggled as we witnessed our children enjoying the fun. Five minutes later, our Reception children were enthusiastically accepting a challenge: Who wants to help unlock the box? They understood what they needed to achieve success and were off...100% were writing, ideas flowed, and children shared their written outcomes confidently...peer assessment followed as they told each other how to upgrade their writing...adjective and conjunctions were added, and again rapid progress was made. Ultimately, the box was open, the contents shared, and a great learning time was had by all. I felt proud of our crowd. We knew the learners had enjoyed themselves because they wanted to know when she was coming back!

On one occasion, I was asked to join the interview panel for a new primary school that were appointing a headteacher. On that occasion, I was asked to supply a dozen or so learners, equipped with questions to lead the student interviews, albeit for another school. The children did a cracking job in their preparation and were well-prepared to run the process. Another local headteacher and I sat back to listen. As each of the three candidates were interviewed by the same group of children asking the same questions, the atmosphere in the room changed dramatically each time. Maybe, you're wondering how that can be when everyone's got the same opportunity? And maybe, you have an idea about what made the greatest difference. Well, one candidate smiled and answered each question well and the interview flowed with everyone in the same business-like state. This was appropriate, of course, and the children received the answers they needed to inform their recommendations to the panel. Another candidate greeted her audience, noted that she was impressed to hear that they were running the process and would love to be their headteacher. After all, they were great ambassadors for their school. As she answered each question, she not only valued the question and noted why she thought it important. She also used the experience to appropriately, lead the learning with embedded questions like: I wonder if my answer has led to anymore questions and if it's okay, I have a few questions to ask you. I'm off to my formal interview next, and I'd really value your help. When the children reflected afterwards, they talked as much about how much they liked a candidate, as they did about their answers to the questions.

Last year, I attended a Neuro-Linguistic Programming Course, in Florida, entitled Persuasion Engineering. The skills in this program teach people how to fine tune language with precision and have real-world application in any business or personal setting. John La Valle, President of the Society of NLP posed the following question to the delegates: What do you sell? Interestingly, everyone said something different and 100% of the class got the answer wrong. I was absolutely sure that I sell learning and when we were eventually told the "right" answer, I couldn't agree more. It turns out that me, a car salesperson, a film director or any other salesperson [for that matter] sells the same thing! And, so do you!

As I prepare to market this book, I've been engaged in a Click Funnell Course that reveals the secrets of online marketing. Part way through the course, I realised that the origin of the strategy is NLP. Russell, Brunson, the CEO, learnt his strategy from Tony Robbins, who learnt his strategy from Richard Bandler. That is to say, that the key learning from the NLP Trainer's Training [Charisma Enhancement] and when I share the key learning, it may well resonate with you in terms of what makes one teacher and/or lesson stand out from another.

In NLP, we acknowledge that our brain codes every experience through the five senses – visual, auditory, kinaesthetic [feeling], gustatory [taste] and olfactory [smell]. When people recall an experience, their language reflects how they've coded the experience.

Take a few moments to reflect back on your own school days. Close your eyes and recall a memorable lesson. Recall what you could see, hear, touch/feel, taste, smell. I wonder what made it memorable and how good [or otherwise] you felt inside. I wonder what made it memorable.

On teaching courses, it's not unusual to be asked to recall a teacher that made a good impression on you, and one that did the opposite! I recall Miss D., a beautiful young teacher from Australia who told us so many stories about living near the bush. Over forty years later, the A-word [Australia] or any of its indigenous species still trigger fond memories of my Year 2 class. Mr McD. taught me when I was 9. He was young, had a gentle voice, took time to circulate and listen to us read back our writing. At the point he was listening, nothing else seemed to matter. He relished our success and would show us how to improve. We got to use binoculars and observe the birds in order to read for information and complete data charts for analysis before writing an explanation about visitors to our school garden. That was a far cry from my teacher the following year who had her favourites and if we didn't learn easily, we were verbally "put-down" and sent to the back of the queue!

When schools ask you to prepare and deliver a lesson, they want to see YOUR supreme art. If they wanted to see your version of somebody else's lesson, they would give you the planning. They're then looking for the Teacher Standards [UK] within the values and ethos of their school. The things that stand out within the infamous "7 second window" in a formal interview, are just as relevant in the classroom. So, you're wise to consider:

1. The remit the school have given you, and what you want for the learners in light of this – not only what you want them to achieve but what you want them and you to see, hear and most importantly FEEL throughout the lesson.

2. How you'll greet the learners to ensure that you get buy-in: How will you hook them? Maintain their attention? Unlock their creative expression and knowledge? And, ensure a memorable learning experience for the RIGHT reasons?

3. What you'll do to secure progress throughout the lesson.

A few weeks ago, I was contacted by Rhianna an enthusiastic and high-flying teacher training student, whose letter of application had secured five interviews, but she hadn't yet landed the job of her dreams. She was confident that the reason why was that she wasn't confident; the feedback she'd been given confirmed this. As did her reflection on the lessons and interviews to date. When she arrived, she put a massive pile of picture books in front of me. The school had asked her to prepare a literacy lesson for Reception and she wanted to start with a book to hook them in. "Which one should I choose?" She asked, flicking through them, "I'm just not sure which one!" There are lots of resources available for The Gruffalo, but everyone does that!" I loved the choice of texts. High quality literature is inspiring after all. What bothered me was that the actual story, wasn't the place to start. Coffee and a coaching chat and she was off! Once she was able to articulate what she wanted for the learner's in terms of learning and engagement [Big Picture], she was able to select a text and use it to create an inspiring hook that the learners would be desperate to achieve. She planned how she would secure buy-in by telling the learners that she had asked the headteacher, could she teach the class with the best ideas and he'd chosen them! Thereafter, she knew what she wanted to secure by the end of the lesson [Beyond the ELG criteria with all learners articulating sentences and recording them confidently]. So, she could now chunk down and plan the detail in order to get there. The coaching questions at the end of this chapter are designed to help you to do the same. Consequently, the lesson was delivered in short episodes that enabled her to track progress every 3 minutes during the 20-minute session. Needless to say, she was confidently able to reflect on progress during the formal interview. In a nutshell, she passed the audition because she owned the show.

So, back to click funnels and persuasion engineering. The secret being that in NLP terms, everything starts and ends with a K [Kinaesthetic]! That is to say, a good feeling. John La Valle, President of the Society of NLP, notes that EVERYONE [Teachers or otherwise] sells FEELINGS and consumers buy products because of the feelings invoked in the sales of advertising process. Richard Bandler, Co-creator of NLP notes that as human beings we love anticipation, and to motivate our audience [or class] we need to build their desire. You know that feeling of anticipation when you have your eye of the ball, a prize or reward, that something you really want. And when you feel the anticipation building inside your belly, that desire grows until you just want to go for it! Thereafter, you do what all human beings do when they've enjoyed themselves…you take a deep breath in and sigh, just like after you've run a race, enjoyed a lovely meal or another joyous pastime! And I'm sure you'll agree that when learning is at its best you move the learners from being curious [about the lesson], to being a little restless [they want to get on with it], to desiring the outcome [wanting to achieve] and then finally going for it!

Now, Richard Brunson who teaches his click funnels strategy to thousands and thousands of people on a daily basis notes the importance of a hook, a story and an offer. I wonder how many of you answered "Yes" to the questions at the start of this chapter. And "yes" a question is oftentimes an excellent hook. Richard Bandler, Tony Robbins, Richard Brunson and the best teachers I know all tell stories that the learners can relate to and put them into the [emotional] states that we want for them to learn well, e.g. curiosity, desire/anticipation, motivation. And when you own the show [lesson plan] you can do that just as well as any other charismatic learning leader. Children, like consumers, know when you like them, and they love to be curious. Maybe, you've brought them something special, or there's a punchline to tell them but not just yet…Ultimately, your ability to have them feeding out of your hands depends on:

1. **Building Rapport:** If they like you, you're halfway there!

2. **Hooking them in:** If your hook invokes curiosity, they'll come with you, so it needs to appeal to their interests, age and stage.

3. **Stories/Stimulus:** If they feel curiosity, hesitation or frustration [maybe a tad restless as you model the learning] anticipation, desire and ultimately, they just want to go for it, you're on a winner.

4. **Derivational search or open loop:** If you leave a story unfinished or a question unanswered, the learner's unconscious mind will keep searching for it; as a result, you're more like to hold their attention because they want to know the answer or be involved.

Rhianna achieved rapport and got buy-in by telling the children that she'd asked to work with the children with the best ideas. Tiddler [the character] was lost and she needed help to find him. 100% were game! The story characters had a few ideas, but she knew theirs would be better. She gave each child an underwater creature [small world toy fish, eels, seahorses, etc] to "perform" with, and invited their ideas.

The children provided the "voices" for the wider characters in the story, who were all happy to write notes to Tiddler. Writing in role enabled all children to contribute in a safe environment. Needless to say, the children loved it and their outcomes were stunning. Why? Because they liked her, they felt good, they wanted to find Tiddler and they succeeded. Maybe, you can imagine the moment when they realised that their messages in a bottle had found their destination.

Rhianna's job winning lesson was resource dependent and many minutes were lost during a rehearsal during one of our coaching sessions. The solution was having group resources "ready to go" via carefully chosen storage that the children could access easily. Without this, the first 5 minutes of her lesson were at risk of showing zero progress.

Some of you may be thinking that's all very well with younger children but the older children are far too old for picture books and you're right, the context must be relevant. As a student of NLP, I continue to learn with the most inspiring teachers who tell stories to support adult states for learning; and of course, they have to get it right for the audience. You may also be thinking that stories have little or no relevance to the subject that you teach and that's okay. If you're teaching a maths lesson, for example, you may use a very different hook to install a good [emotional] state for learning. Kate Benson, International Director of Education for the Society of NLP creates curiosity by putting a gift bag in the room with the suggestion: Don't look in the bag! It's a reverse suggestion so her students go to look in the bag and then stop in their tracks. She also tells quick stories to set the scene and will open a story loop by saying something like, "Something amazing happened to me on my way here...I'll tell you about it later, if we have time." By opening the loop, she's created curiosity and has the attention of her class. She can then teach away and close the loop at a pertinent moment in the lesson. In the meantime, the students are apt to remain curious and motivated and are likely to ask: When can we look in the bag? This is because a loop has been opened and their brain wants to keep searching for the information.

Teaching clients who approach me for job coaching, often ask me what format they should use for presenting their lesson plan. My answer is always the same. Use the format that works for you! In terms of the magic ingredients mentioned at the start of this chapter, it's important to note that Dr Richard Bandler, Co-creator of NLP, teaches his students about the nature of the human beast. That is to say, we all do what we do to get a good feeling. Next time you're eating, playing a game, exercising, enjoying a drink, a hug or something else you really like, notice that when you're finished you breathe in and sigh...and it feels so good. Your students inevitably do the same at key points in their learning, not least when they finish an outcome. So, now you know your supreme art as a teacher, I wonder what you will do to awaken a [good] feeling of joy [or enjoyment] in creative expression and knowledge?

The following exercise enables you to use the 4Mat Method that I was introduced to when I became a valued member of the training support team for Richard Bander. I share is because we are required to teach adult students key NLP Concepts, Skills and Techniques in just 18 – 20 mins. This strategy works best when trainers get their students into a good state and students know what's in it for them from the onset. You can then decide how you'll measure progress every 3-5 minutes and build in more challenge as appropriate to the needs of the learners. The timings and impact on the quick plan sheet provided work for me, to ensure that milestones in learning are achieved at a rapid pace. The purpose of this challenge is to support you to plan specifically for progress in your interview lesson, without falling into the trap of over planning.

The 4Mat model was originally developed by Bernice McCarthy in the 1980s and reflected the four different styles of learners put forward by David Kolb. The 4Mat Model is informed by research on the findings of learning styles, including right and left-brain dominance. It includes right brain[creative] and left brain [logical] strategies, within four distinct phases of the learning cycle:

1. **Experiencing** [Feeling – Innovative Learners]

2. **Conceptualising** [Thinking – Analytic Learners]

3. **Applying** [Doing – Common Sense Learners]

4. **Refining** [Reflecting – Dynamic Learners]

As teachers or trainers, it gives us a systematic way to enable all students to think and learn well.

Exercise 1:

Follow the 4 Mat Method to plan progress for ALL types of learners

As you plan each episode, consider what you or the learners will say or do, to ensure their enjoyment in creative expression or knowledge building. The "Overview and Purpose" model below suggest a 20-minute input; you can adjust the timings accordingly so that:

1. **Innovative Learners:** Know WHY they are learning
   [Share purpose; what's in it for them]

2. **Analytic Learners:** Know WHAT [facts] they need & answer, "What?"
   [Model/teach knowledge & skills]

3. **Common Sense Learners:** Know HOW to apply what they know to the real world [Coach application]

4. **Dynamic Learners:** Know WHERE else learning can be applied and answer "What if" [Facilitate thinking]

Top Tip: You may like to think about each quadrant being a new episode in the lesson when learning moves forward.

4 Mat Lesson Plan Model – Proforma	
Quadrant 1: Why? [2 mins] **Goal – ENGAGE:** Facilitate learner to get involved, giving meaning to the subject, visualising and allowing them to integrate aspects of the subject; in relation to them and their context. **Connect [Right Brain – Creative]** • Link learning to the question, "Why?" • How? Get the learner to think about or share personal experience. **Attend [Left Brain – Logical]** • Discussion: Have students examine the experience, looking beyond their own experience.	**Quadrant 2: What? [4 mins]** **Goal – SHARE:** Present information that enables the learners to: Conceptualise, define, shape and acquire knowledge. **Image [Right Brain – Creative]** • Enable students to picture/see the subject material. • Reinforce their focus by modelling and/or using visual resources **Inform [Left Brain – Logical]** • Model/teach key learning, core skills or information linked to the shared learning experience [N.B. This should lead to further application or research by the learners]
Quadrant 3: How? [10 mins] **Goal-PRACTICE:** Coach learners to apply and demonstrate the learning that they have just received. **Practice [Left Brain – Logical]** • Learners complete activities that enable them to apply their developing knowledge and skills logically, e.g. worksheet or framework provided. **Extend [Right Brain – Creative]** • Learners contribute their own thinking and ideas, approaching the main content of the lesson in their own way, e.g. collecting data, answering questions, investigating, making decisions.	**Quadrant 4: What if/else? [4 mins]** **Goal – EVALUATE:** Facilitate learners to answer the what if/else question by identifying any limitations, reviewing, closing, evaluating and/or summarising **Refine [Left Brain – Logical]** • Learners analyse what they have learnt, noting where else they can use their transferable knowledge and/or skills. **Perform [Right Brain – Creative]** • Learners explain to each other what they have learned or created. • Learners answer questions about what they have gained from the entire lesson/experience.

4 Mat Lesson Plan Model – Proforma

Context: NLP Practitioner Training – Carousel of Learning

Learning Objective: To teach the NLP Tools of State and enable all learners to apply their learning

Audience: 6 groups of 40

Trainers: Tanya and Xavi

Episode 1: Why? [2 mins]	Episode 2: What? [4 mins]
ENGAGE **Connect [Right Brain – Creative]** Hook by Tanya [Universal metaphor: It's something that they can all relate to] *I wonder if you've ever tried to complete a task that became impossible because you just weren't in the right frame of mind?* **Impact:** Students have to think about it and represent the memory in their mind. **Attend [Left Brain – Logical]** *Wouldn't it be great to be able to control your own state, so that you can lead others to be in the right emotional state for the task in hand?* [Clear purpose] **Impact:** Students recognise the purpose in what they are learning.	**SHARE** **Image [Right Brain – Creative]** • Demo [Xavi]: Tell "Stepping in Dog Poo" story to elicit FRUSTRATION. • Demo [Tanya]: Tell "I'm gonna play the Gruffalo" to elicit EXCITEMENT. • Visual resource: States Poster – Bored, Sad, Tense, Ease, Cross, Curious, Happy, etc. **Inform [Left Brain – Logical]** Task/Challenge: 1. Watch and guess the state. 2. Be ready to say what skills we used to elicit the states effectively. Impact: Students can name tools of state. 3. Record ideas [Elicit success criteria]: Voice, gesture, movement, posture, words, intonation, pause, content, expression, etc. **Teaching Points:** • Pace and lead: Change your state and your audience will follow. • Calibrate: Notice if audience state changes and be flexible, as necessary.

4 Mat Lesson Plan Model – Proforma

Context: NLP Practitioner Training – Carousel of Learning

Learning Objective: To teach the NLP Tools of State and enable all learners to apply their learning

Audience: 6 groups of 40

Trainers: Tanya and Xavi

Episode 3: How? [10 mins/5 mins each]	Episode 4: What if/else? [4 mins]
PRACTICE: Practice [Left Brain – Logical]	**EVALUATE: Refine [Left Brain – Logical]**
Round 1 [2.5 mins each]	• Learners analyse what they have learnt, noting where else they can use their transferable knowledge and/or skills: Acting, teaching, etc.
• Partner 1: Tell a story that elicits one or two states.	
• Partner 2: Guess the state	**Perform [Right Brain – Creative]**
• Swop roles and repeat	• Learners explain to each other what they have learned or created.
Round 2 [2.5 mins each] Challenge: Tell a story that creates a number/chain of different states, e.g. ecstasy, despair and back again, or something similar!	• Learners answer questions about what they have gained from the entire lesson/experience.
	Challenge: Were there any other tools of state that you noticed?
Extend [Right Brain – Creative]	
• Use the success criteria to give your partner feedback.	**Teaching Point:** Link to RB on stage. Quote: *If you don't go into the right state, you don't get the right result. If you don't feel a bit of tension, you won't sound tense.*
• Note one or two highlights that affected your state change and justify one area for development.	
	Impact: Learner's own their learning about how to transfer their NLP skills.
Continuous assessment: Tanya and Xavi notice student's skills in eliciting/changing states quickly. Prompt/coach/support/celebrate!	
Impact: Accelerated progress – Students articulate the difference that makes the difference.	

4 Mat Lesson Plan Model – Proforma	
Episode 1: Why?	**Episode 2: What?**
Episode 3: How?	**Episode 4: What if/else?**

Key Points

★ Be quick to build rapport with your audience/class, e.g. introduce yourself and make sure that they know why you're happy to be teaching them.

★ Tell a story or do something else that quickly puts all learners into a good [emotional] state for learning.

★ Be congruent: Show that you mean what you are saying. If your body language doesn't match, the learners will smell a rat!

★ Plan to meet the needs of different types of learners, remembering that to get a good feeling we all need to access the learning in the right way for us and know our questions are being answered [4Mat: Why? What? How? What else/if?]

★ Know the progress that you want the learners to make so that you and they can track progress towards it.

★ Celebrate progress as it happens; whoever, is conducting the lesson observation will be tuned into your voice and will notice progress when you celebrate it.

★ Be prepared: Consider how you and the students will access resources easily throughout the lesson to avoid time slippage and show great organisational skills.

*It's important to note that we don't all learn in just one way all of the time; it's simply that different learners show preferences and can "flow" with their learning when they feel and know their needs are being met.

8

Create an Authentic, Professional & Confident Image

How to dress, pose and present for success!

"Elegance is not standing out but being remembered."
GIORGIO ARMANI

"I firmly believe that with the right footwear one can rule the world."
BETTE MIDLER

★ I wonder if you've ever got dressed to go somewhere and ended up changing because it just didn't feel or look right?

★ Or, worn something that you've later regretted because you hadn't realised there was a dress code?

★ Maybe, you've noticed someone else at an important event who just didn't look comfortable?

Wouldn't it be great to know that your choice of attire was just right for your teacher interview? You do want to dress for success, don't you?

In this chapter, I tell a few stories for you to consider when choosing your interview outfit and share a few top tips to ensure that you look and feel your best for the task in hand.

Back in 2001, I was a teaching deputy at an amazing school in a pocket of high deprivation on the South Coast. I was in my element, teaching a reception class of little people with HUGE personalities! Pupil voice was just becoming a thing, so one day after a fun plenary I asked my class what I could do to be an even better teacher. Lacey, aged 4, shot up from the floor and exclaimed, "You can wear an animal dress and animal shoes, and an animal belt!" Enjoying the moment, I promised that I would one day when the time was right. The following Summer was the Queen's Golden Jubilee and I was tasked with arranging a 1950s Carnival. My class would lead the street parade and we would all be dressed in 1950s attire. Needless to say, I was bowled over when Lacie and her best friend's grown ups co-ordinated matching outfits so that they out dressed John Travolta and Olivia Newton-John. My stunning rocking rollers would win everyone's heart. My only dilemma now was what could I wear to fit the bill? It would have to be good enough for Lacey and that was a tall order!

As a headteacher, I resisted having a staff dress code for years; not least because I love individuality. However, over the years a few things happened that caused me to rethink my stance. I remember one fine day when I parked my car and walked into the school entrance, listening to somebody beeping their horn. My PA recognised the vehicle outside, jumped up from her desk and opened the window. A parent [Dad] who was now standing on the rocker panel of his van so that he could see over the top, was shouting, "Who's that?" As I walked into the main office, my PA was shouting back, "It's the new headteacher!" The Dad replied, enthusiastically, "Phwarrrh…They didn't look like that in my day!" You may well be wondering what I was wearing and whether that's what caused his reaction. I'll leave it your to imagination, for now. Needless to say, this parental response did make me think!

As you now know, I often used to say that headteachers get the best jobs and most of the time I was being serious. There were, however, a few occasions when I wished the ground would swallow me up. School tours for prospective new families are times when you want to feel proud of your crowd and nothing else. I remember one occasion when my Year 6 ambassadors were leading a tour, and someone enquired about their gold ties. They waxed lyrical about the privilege of wearing a gold tie, as ambassadors, and noted how pride linked with our core value of respect. Someone commented on how smart we all looked, and we continued, with wind in our sails, down to the Early Years annexe. On entering, the first reception classroom we were greeted by a bejazzled whale tail [thong] and a teaching version of a builder's bum. The teacher in question was certainly down with the children and leading learning with a group at their level. The children were enjoying their learning and I did have to wonder how many of our visitors were enjoying the view, or not. When the teacher stood up to introduce herself, she did attempt to adjust her clothing accordingly so that with a full frontal we were only aware of nothing less than a G-cup and a jewelled tummy button. Note to self that night was, reconsider staff dress code asap! I'd seen a few short skirts and transparent leggings of late and this was nearly the final straw, but not quite!

As I prepared for an upcoming INSET day, I thought carefully about how I would consult with school staff with regard to the dress code and referred to an earlier copy of the best practice guidelines that follow. I respected my staff and wanted them to be happy.

At a recent NLP Practitioner Training, Kathleen La Valle, Master Trainer of NLP, noted how our clothes can be anchors. Anchoring is deliberately connecting a cue or trigger to a state of mind so that you can recall the state simply and easily later. I certainly have some lucky boots that have secured a few proud performances, not to mention two headships! They are beautiful calf leather, mid-heel shoe/boots [ankle height] that I feel good and walk well in. They look great with a suit and were therefore suitable for interview. Needless to say, that because I feel confident in them, that's what

---

8. Dress and appearance

A person's dress and appearance are matters of personal choice and self-expression and some individuals will wish to exercise their own cultural customs. However, staff should select a manner of dress and appearance appropriate to their professional role and which may be necessarily different to that adopted in their personal life. Staff should ensure they are dressed decently, safely and appropriately for the tasks they undertake. Those who dress or appear in a manner which could be viewed as offensive or inappropriate will render themselves vulnerable to criticism or allegation.

This means that staff should wear clothing which:
- *promotes a positive and professional image*
- *is appropriate to their role*
- *is not likely to be viewed as offensive, revealing, or sexually provocative*
- *does not distract, cause embarrassment or give rise to misunderstanding*
- *is absent of any political or otherwise contentious slogans*
- *is not considered to be discriminatory*
- *is compliant with professional standards*

Source: Guidance for safer working practice for those working with children and young people in education settings, DfES September 2015

my audience see. Richard Bandler, teaching NLP Practitioners about tools of state at the same recent seminar noted, "If you want to sound tense, you have to feel a little tense." Conversely, if you want to look and sound confident, you have to feel a little confidence! Now, I'm not saying that confidence comes simply from what you're wearing but it is an important factor, especially if your clothes have a detrimental effect for you or cause your audience to question your professionalism.

On that note, two specific colleagues come to mind. The first, a male teacher attending interview who was far more at ease when he took off his frock coat. He later admitted to me that it was an impulse buy and it just wasn't him. Another was a female teacher who wore a cream blouse with a smart navy shift style dress, business style jacket and low court shoes. She looked confidently and comfortable when teaching without the jacket, and a true professional with the jacket on for the formal interview. So much so that the interview panel made special mention of her authentic, professional and confident image. Interview panels aren't always so kind and the following comments are genuine remarks that I've heard over the years, during panel deliberations. I wonder what impact they'll have on you and how you want to be remembered.

*"Everything we **saw** and heard SHOUTED a true professional."* [Visual]

*"Wow. What a **smart** young man in every sense of the word. Shame about the carrier bag!"* [Visual]

*"I **liked** how he said that he would always wear a tie, not least because if the children had to wear a tie it was the least he could do."* [Kinaesthetic]

*"Well **presented**. An excellent role model for our whole school team."* [Visual]

*"Amazing attention to detail, from how she **looked, walked, talked**. I **feel** she'll be a great ambassador for our school. That's how we want all our staff to look."* [Visual, Auditory, Kinaesthetic]

*"He was quietly confident throughout. I **felt comfortable** that he'll do a good job."* [Kinaesthetic]

*"I felt she knew her audience; her presentation **hit the spot**. She got everything just right."* [Kinaesthetic]

*"I was constantly **distracted** by the scrunchie being taken off and played with throughout."* [Visual]

*"The shoes **looked** perfect for the night club."* [Visual]

*"Bless... Did you **see** he still had the price label on his shoes?"* [Visual]

*"I'm sorry [laughs] but I couldn't take her seriously in the **Minnie Mouse shoes**..."* [Visual]

*"I know the lesson remit was PE, but you'd have **thought** a collar and tie for the formal interview was a no brainer."* [Visual image]

"Was anyone else distracted when she put her boobs on the table. I know she's got to put them somewhere but really? [Visual]

*"The **squeaky** shoes drove me nuts. If he's stood still, it wouldn't have been quite so bad."* [Auditory]

*"His answers were technically sound, but the **hesitant voice** and **body language** tells me that our students will make mincemeat of him."* [Auditory/Visual]

As you consider each comment and notice the impression that is has on you, you'll also notice the words in bold. In the NLP world, these are called predicates. Predicates are words and phrases that we all use that show our current or preferred representation system. That is to say, the sensory system [Visual, Auditory, Kinaesthetic, Olfactory or Gustatory] where we code our experience. In a nutshell, the words we use reflect how we think and experience our world. So, as you plan carefully what to wear you can remember your audience.

Key Learning: How you look and feel at interview affects both you and your audience. What they see and hear in the interview room affects how they feel about you. Ultimately, it's your reputation and job offer that's at stake. So, it's good to consider how you want to be remembered, don't you think?

Will you dress to impress? Dress for confidence? Comfort? Or all three?

And, how do you know the dress code if nobody tells you?

Further to what you wear, your professional stance [posture] is also important. Professor Amy Cuddy is an American Psychologist who wondered whether our physicality [Body Posture] affects our Psychology [Mood and Confidence]. So, she carried out extensive research to find out by having subjects pose in low body poses [Imagine Eeyore who is painfully shy] compared to Wonder Woman [Fierce and Fantastic]! Professor Cuddy's investigations proved that our physiology does affect our neurology for better or worse. So, using power poses of your choice on a daily basis on the run up to your interview will give you an increasing sense of confidence and well-being, as necessary.

Going back to my teaching staff dress code that we discussed on a staff training day when the pressure was off. I wanted staff to be informed and own whatever we agreed, so rather than telling them what to wear I circulated various pieces of research and guidance including information from the Health and Safety Executive, as well as some examples from other schools. The staff then suggested wording for the dress code, and I scribed until Sally [one of our resident comedians] noticed the Secret Agenda...

"*So, what you want, Tanya,*" she said, knowing full well that consultation isn't really negotiation, "*Is 5Ts...*"

Her timing was brilliant. The whole room stopped, looked and gave her full attention as she summarised our new dress code in just five words...

"*No tits, tums, toes, thongs or tattoos!*"

Needless to say, from that day forward and from my point of view as a headteacher, it was a win/win situation. The few staff who had been pushing the professional boundaries not only dressed appropriately; they retained autonomy over their personal style and did it with a smile.

I realised how much our audience [the children/students] value and notice personal style on one occasion when I returned from a family wake in Dublin. During the trip, I had treated myself to a cropped hair do [complete restyle] and the quirkiest business jacket and boots that I just adored. Over lunchtime, I had a meeting with our Year 6 ambassadors who admired my new outfit. I thanked them, noting that nobody had mentioned my hair. "No," said one of the students. "That's because we liked your bun!"

That day, just like the Lacey days, somebody, albeit a student did tell me the dress code! And I recall another occasion when "walking the talk" with my impeccable Deputy Headteacher. As the children filed into assembly, she was catching them being good. Every now and again, between the positive affirmations she reminded children to "Tuck your shirt in", as necessary. One day, I recall walking passed her to lead the assembly and tucking in my designer shirt tails accordingly!

And, sometimes, even headteachers need to rethink. As it happens, the day the Dad shouted, "Phwoah...", I was actually wearing my version of business attire – a white fitted blouse, pin stripped fitted crops, a neat double-breasted jacket and neat black shoes. One of the presuppositions of NLP notes that, "The meaning of all communication is the response you get." This includes, non-verbal communication so how you dress shouldn't cause freak-out but requires thought, so that you boost your chances with your audience – the class you teach, the student council and the interview panel; as well as anyone else you come into contact with. Needless to say, I didn't wear the "Phwarr" outfit again; my version of business attire or not, it wasn't a communication that got an appropriate response. At the end of the day, I was the main role and had to lead by example if I wanted my staff to follow suit. I'm not saying that you should dress like the headteacher but paying attention when you view the school and reflecting the highest standards that you've seen in your own apparel will have an impact.

Exercise 1
Research

Research what dress code is suitable for your interview and plan your "wardrobe" in advance to avoid a last-minute rush.

Exercise 2
Watch

Watch the famous Ted Talk by Professor Amy Cuddy and begin to practise those daily power poses that will make the biggest difference to you.

Key Points

★ Dress for success by choosing an outfit that you feel confident and comfortable in.

★ Notice what other professionals in the school are wearing and aim to dress a notch above the students; if they're smart, you can be even smarter!

★ Dress for the task, whatever that may be and if you're delivering a practical lesson [Art, Drama or Physical Education], do dress appropriately for the formal interview.

★ Reflect on your own confidence and posture and begin to practise daily power poses as appropriate to you.

★ Remember that your appearance can be positively or negatively affected by the accessories you choose. If you've got resources to carry, ensure that they're packed appropriately and anything you need is easily accessible.

9

Imagine Your Best Performance Yet...

How to be confident when the spotlight's on you!

"I get stage fright and gremlins in my head, saying: You're going to forget your lines."

ALAN RICKMAN, ACTOR

"I get shitty scared. I've thrown up a couple of times. Once in Brussels, I projectile-vomited on someone. I just gotta bear it. But I don't like touring. I have anxiety attacks a lot."

ADELE, SINGER

"I was on 'Strictly' because I was getting stage fright. I was taught that I had to imagine what a good outcome would be and be happy with it."

RACHEL RILEY, PRESENTER

★ Have you ever wondered why it is that some people suffer with performance anxiety, whilst others appear to sail through?

★ Maybe, you're confident with some people, yet nervous with others?

★ Or perhaps, you've completed your interview preparation, but you're worried about how well you'll perform on the day?

Wouldn't it be wonderful to know how we create our fears and learn effective ways to invoke positive feelings in good time for your interview performance?

In this chapter, I share more of the lessons learnt by Rhianna, a recent NQT client who had begun to think that she was never going to be the successful candidate. Rhianna was referred to me by a colleague, who noted that my experience was better suited to supporting a positive outcome. As you know from Chapter 7, Rhianna's letter had secured no less than five interviews and she was on track for a First-Class Honours Degree with Qualified Teacher Status.

On arrival for interview coaching, Rhianna came in smiling and excited. My first impression was that she was a bundle of fun, who would light up any classroom. Rhianna spoke rapidly about her upcoming [fifth] interview. She had lots of ideas and couldn't wait to start planning her lesson and completing a mock interview with me! I was slightly taken aback because my understanding was that Rhianna wanted support with performance anxiety and suddenly a double breakthrough session [2 hours] was turning into three! Rhianna kept talking nineteen to the dozen, until I stopped her in order to find out exactly what she wanted. Whilst I didn't fault her enthusiasm, if she presented interview in the same non-stop chatting mode, she would exhaust the interview panel and completely confuse them!

When she slowed down, Rhianna noted that she wanted to get a teaching job and had two more interviews coming up. However, she didn't think she would get either job because everyone that had given her feedback, to date,

noted confidence as an issue.

"I'm just rubbish at interviews," she told me.

Rhianna's negative belief had been reinforced each and every time she was rejected. This limiting belief was now so strong that she even asked me, "Tanya, as an ex-headteacher, do you think I'll ever get a job?"

Like many other Newly Qualified Teachers [NQTs], Rhianna's track record including lesson observations, an excellent reference and a high-quality degree, suggested that she could fulfil the job description; she just hadn't managed to be the successful candidate yet. My hunch or mindread was that she had little experience and had yet to hone her interview skills; a bit like myself all those years ago…

As for confidence or feeling nervous, various research suggests that approximately 25% of the population have a fear of public speaking; so, it's not surprising that this translates to the interview context. Having led the recruitment process myself, for the best part of twenty years, I would say that 1:4 being greatly affected is realistic, and that everyone is likely to be affected to a greater or lesser extent at some point throughout the process.

So, what causes "interview anxiety" and how is it that some candidates not only manage their fears but excel at being in a positive and resourceful state, even when faced by the most probing and ferocious interview panel?

As Rhianna reflected on her recent interview and the feedback given, I watched her re-run the memories and as she recalled the "movie in her mind" her emotional and physical state transformed in front of me. That bundle of fun that I'd opened the door to was gone, her colour drained, her body posture sank, her breathing shallowed and her eyes welled. She was totally gripped by doubt. As a NLPer, my observations showed me that she was either recalling or creating [negative] pictures in her mind about the interview process, to date. Furthermore, I could see from following her eye accessing cues that her internal dialogue was far from good.

The cause of interview anxiety for Rhianna was unique to her. Her recent disappointment had caused self-doubt and she was now questioning her own ability to the extent that in her mind she could see things going wrong again and this was resulting in a certain amount of self-sabotage, despite the fact that the quality of her preparation told me that she was a well-prepared candidate. In my experience, this isn't always the case and interview nerves can stem from a range of factors including but not limited to:

1. **Limiting beliefs**, e.g. *"I'm just rubbish at interviews...Everyone says I need to be more confident."*

2. **Imagining the worst:** Seeing a negative picture in your mind, e.g. the moment when something goes wrong. Remember Rhianna, who imagined herself having little or no confidence.

3. **Negative self-talk:** Telling yourself what will go wrong or questioning your ability to do the job well.

Whilst it's normal for all of us to feel nervous from time to time, Performance and/or Social Anxiety become an issue when your fears stop you from securing the job you want.

One of the presuppositions of Neuro-Linguistic Programming [NLP] is that "...there is a positive intention behind every behaviour." This includes conscious and unconscious behaviours, whether you know the intention or not. As a Clinical Hypnotherapist, I sometimes work with my clients to find the root cause of their behaviour; finding that oftentimes the presenting symptoms [e.g. fear, blushing, sweating, heart racing, panic attacks, dissociation, or similar] are the result of an unpleasant experience in the past. Some clients can name their fears, whilst others tell me that they're no longer sure of the trigger and that the symptoms come on all of a sudden. That is to say, that people's experience of Anxiety can vary considerably and so can finding the solution. However, with some key knowledge and a few easy to learn techniques, you can begin to take back control of your emotional state and be prepared for your interview today.

As humans, we're hardwired to be anxious. If I reframe that and state it in the positive, you're hard wired to keep yourself safe.

Autonomic Nervous System [ANS]

The ANS has two parts:
1. Sympathetic Nervous System [SNS]
2. Parasympathetic Nervous System [PNS]

The role of the SNS is to prepare the body to defend itself by activating glands and organs. This is called the Fight or Flight response. Blood flow to the brain and muscles is increased, whilst blood flow to non-essential muscles/organs such as the digestive system is decreased. The adrenal glands are activated to provide us with the energy to run or fight. This is crucial for survival when there is a genuine risk. This is how Neolithic man could escape from a bear!

The PNS is concerned with healing, nourishing and regeneration of the body. It stimulates the immune system, digestion and organs that promote wellbeing. The parasympathetic nervous system can be activated by relaxation, rest and positive thoughts.

Fact or Fiction?

The issue with any form of anxiety is that it activates the Sympathetic Nervous System even when the fear isn't really there. Our body copes with this in small doses, for example, when we watch a scary film but if the PNS is constantly preparing us to fight, run or freeze we start to feel tired and run down. In Rhianna's case, her first attempt at a mock interview question showed that her fear or self-doubt, revealed by her question, "Have I said the right answer?" and subsequent comment, "I know this, I just can't think", revealed that her self-doubt [negative thoughts] were affecting her emotional state [Stage/Interview fright].

The Key to Managing Your Performance Anxiety

If you can activate the parasympathetic state, you can pre-empt or reverse the symptoms of anxiety. The two systems can't work at the same time, and you can use a good feeling to outweigh anything else. When it comes to interviews, a certain amount of stress or anxiety can be good. Eustress refers to the beneficial aspects of stress, e.g. the anxious or stressful feeling that propels you to prepare well for your interview and complete a mock interview.

Richard Bandler, Co-Creator of NLP, explains that as humans we think in words and pictures. Words and pictures are powerful because they trigger good or bad feelings; thus, activating the nervous system. In a nutshell, if someone is scared of a picture in their head [e.g. Sweating, panicking or not being able to answer the interview question] they activate the ANS because they're scared of the thought. Basically, it's the worrying about a negative outcome that becomes the issue. This means that if you can learn to change the pictures and sounds that you make in your head, you can learn to change your response in order to excel at interview and secure your job offer. Exercise works on the principle of Reciprocal Inhibition advocated by the Behaviourist, Joseph Wolpe. Dr Richard Bandler puts this in simple terms when he notes that, "You can't be in two [emotional] states at once...A good feeling will always outweigh a bad one!" Anchoring is a key skill that Dr Bandler developed and teaches on the NLP Practitioner Course. This skill is fundamental to a number of NLP change techniques that are used widely in the coaching world to enable client success. The term, "Super State" anchor was coined by Debbie Williams, NLP Trainer and Clinical Hypotherapist, who utilises this strategy when teaching clients to build positive habits.

The NLP Swish Pattern works by replacing negative pictures or sounds with positive ones. You can use it to change an unwanted behaviour [e.g. panic] into a positive behaviour [e.g. confidence] by changing the sub modalities [pictures or sounds] that are often linked with a trigger [e.g. interview nerves] or cue image [imagining the worst].

The exercises below supported Rhianna to replace her unwanted behaviours as part of the final coaching session that preceded her successful interview. They were learnt consciously and then sealed in trance. You can achieve the behaviour changes that are appropriate for you by following the simple steps below and listening to the tracks on the Tanya Bunting Coaching Hypnosis Download,

"A Trance to Shine at Interview".

At this point, I'm reminded of a question that Dr Bandler always asks his clients or demo subjects when they realise the negative pictures or sounds that they've been creating. He asks them, "Is that smart?" And of course, they know that it's not. Once you learn how to take control of your thoughts, you can be smart and use them to better effect. After her thorough preparation both in and out of trance, Rhianna performed confidently at interview noting in her review...

Tanya Bunting
Hypnotherapy and NLP

> I strongly recommend Tanya Bunting Coaching for anyone who is applying for a teaching interview or a new job. After being unsuccessful at interview, my confidence was knocked. I worried that I might never get a teaching job. After working with Tanya who coached me through the entire process from lesson preparation, to delivery and formal interview, I left feeling confident and ready to take on my next interview. Throughout the interview day, I felt calm and confident as I undertook the various tasks including a lesson observation, planning task, marking and the formal interview. I was the last one to interview and they called me soon after I got into my car to leave. I was really excited to let Tanya know that I'd accepted the job.

Exercise 1
Establish an NLP "Super State" anchor

Purpose: To put yourself quickly into a positive emotional state for the interview process.
How? Remember the Increasing Confidence Activity [Chapter 3, Exercise 2, Step 2]. This time you're going to STACK YOUR ANCHOR so that you can re-access all of those good feelings to support your best state for the interview process.

1. Think of three to four positive emotions that you want to support your emotional state for the interview process, e.g. 1. Confidence, 2. Pride, 3. Calm, 4. Humour [Giggle]

2. Close your eyes. Remember a time when you were **confident** in the past. In the words of Paul McKenna, "See what you saw, hear what you heard and feel what you felt as you *relive that confident memory* all over again". And as you do, notice that good feeling inside. Speed up that confident feeling and anchor it by squeezing your thumb and middle finger.

3. Break state. Think of something unrelated, e.g. what you had for breakfast.

4. Test your anchor.

5. Repeat twice more for emotion 1, e.g. Confidence, so that you stack those good feelings; anchoring or saving them within your neurology so that you can fire off those good feelings by squeezing your thumb and middle finger, when you need them again in the future.

6. Repeat steps 1-5 for the further positive emotions that you want to create, e.g. 2. Pride, 3. Calm, 4. Humour [Giggle].

Exercise 2
NLP – Visual Swish Pattern

[Use this when you know you have a cue picture that triggers unwanted feelings]

1. Identify the interview behaviour that you want to change.

2. Notice the cue image that starts the process [Current state]

3. Notice the positive intention of the undesired state; maybe you are shy at interview because you're unconscious is protecting you from embarrassing yourself.

4. Identify a new image, so that you see yourself behaving in a resourceful way. Make sure that this new picture satisfies the positive intention [e.g. protection] of the undesired state.

5. Imagine the undesired picture/state. Notice the colour, size and shape of the picture. Try changing the colour, size or shape of the picture and notice how you can decrease your desire for the unwanted behaviour. This can often be achieved by changing the colours to black and white and shrinking the picture. Conversely, you can use the same sub modalities to increase your confidence to achieve the new/desired state or behaviour.

6. Bring up picture 1 [Undesired behaviour]. Generally, this will be a "life size" image in your mind.

7. Insert, a mini picture 2 [Desired behaviour] in the bottom left hand corner.

8. Count to three and swish the pictures so that the unwanted "life sized" picture shrinks to a "dot" and is replace by the wanted picture [desired behaviour] Repeat x6. Work quickly because your brain likes to work quickly, and this will enable the change to stick! When you swop the pictures in your mind as quickly as you can say the word "Swish", you'll know you're doing it right.

9. Make the colours of the desired [behaviour] picture big, bright and focused.

10. If you're looking at the picture, step into it so that you are fully associated. Notice how much better you feel now and the good resources that are now available.

11. Increase/spin the good feelings and anchor those, just as you did in the "Increasing Confidence" activity in Chapter 3.

12. Test. Notice what happens now when you try to bring up the original cue picture. It's tricky, isn't it? That's because you've installed your new and wanted behaviour.

Exercise 3
NLP – Auditory Swish Pattern

[Use this when you are repeating your negative self-talk]

1. Notice your negative voice/utterances. Note the side/ear that you can hear.

2. Make a mental note of want to hear instead.

3. Imagine the sound control in your mind. Metaphor: You may be able to visualise a sound deck with two sliders, just like those used by a sound engineer.

4. The slider that's "up" right now operates the negative voice; the old voice that you want to change.

5. The new or motivating voice is on the other slider; the one that's turned down. That's the one you can hear in your other ear!

6. Swish your voice: Start off with the old voice. As the old voices begins its negative utterance, turn that slider down and the new voice up so that you hear what you want to hear instead.

7. Repeat this how ever many times it takes for the new voice to come in automatically. Top-tip: Persevere and work quickly to install the change and ensure it sticks!

Key Points

Remember:

★ **Fears are often created in our imagination; they may be rooted in a past experience or because caused by us letting our mind run riot!**

★ **If you change the negative pictures and/or words; you change the associated feelings so that you can achieve.**

★ **Work systematically through the exercises above and listen to the download, "A Trance to Shine at Interview".**

10

Treading the boards on your interview stage...

How to pay attention to the details that make the difference "backstage" and in the spotlight.

"Keep your eye on the prize."
—DR RICHARD BANDLER

"Nothing is impossible.
The word itself says, I'm possible!
—ANONYMOUS

★ I wonder if you've ever experienced a situation where you've been distracted or tired and looked back, only to realise that you'd said or done something differently?

★ Wouldn't it be wonderful always to respond appropriately?

★ And, communicate so well that you talk yourself into the job?

Interviews can be one of those occasions when although you want to take responsibility for your own actions and get everything right, it's easy to be "thrown" by the pressure of the situation and the behaviour of others. In this chapter, I support you to remember to pay attention, mind your language and manage your emotional state to be successful.

Looking back on my own experience as an interviewee, I'm reminded of times when I wished I'd been ahead of the game. On one such occasion, I was being interviewed for my first teaching job. After the formal interview, I found myself in the staffroom having coffee with the Chair of Governors who wasn't on the interview panel. She was friendly and enquired about all sorts of things, including questions about my new-born baby. As a proud new Mum, I found it easy to wax lyrical and then gulped when I realised that her next port of call was a discussion with the interview panel!

I also remember being in full flow during my interview for deputy headship when my attention was drawn to the non-verbal cues of a local authority inspector. Initially, he raised his eyebrows, so I kept on talking until he frowned, took a slow intake of breath and finally gestured for me to "wind it down"! I realised afterwards that he was on my side and didn't want me talking myself out of a job!

Thinking logical levels, it was in this same interview that the interview panel reflected on my application and asked me to explain a comment that stated, "...the environment has to be right for me and my class to excel". Unfortunately, I had only considered the physical aspects of the environment and was "thrown" when the panel requested my response to the human elements.

In my experience, it's also not unusual for candidates to affect the emotional state of each other, whilst awaiting their formal interview. On one such occasion, I recall a candidate who was upset about his performance and carried out a full "post-mortem" in the waiting room.

He noted the questions he was asked, how he'd them answered and then systematically quizzed the other candidates. Thus, starting a debate between the headship candidates about specific questions and what might be the job winning answers! As you can imagine, this caused a range of emotions amongst the interviewees, including:

★ **Panic:** Did I answer that question correctly? Heck, what shall I say when they ask me?

★ **Agitation:** Is it really any of your business what happened in "my" interview?

★ **Paranoia:** Have they asked us all the same questions and why did they quiz me more?

To name but a few!

And then there was the headship interview when the male chair of governors came out to invite me into my interview, took a double take and asked if we'd met before. At first, I couldn't remember and asked him where he'd lived and gone to school. His answer brought the memory back and we entered the interview room with me cheekily saying, "I was the girl next door"! Needless to say, that if the Chair of Governors hadn't explained the situation to his colleagues, they may have found me a tad too familiar!

So, what can you do to focus and ensure that all communications are appropriate and well received?

1. Be aware that 100% of the school personnel may have been asked to host your visit and been required to advise the panel of any feedback that they deem appropriate.

2. Pay attention on the outside so that you hear what is said and calibrate [measure] your audience to gauge their feedback. Adjust your answers accordingly.

3. Reread your own application prior to the formal interview and ensure that you can explain any probing questions regarding any aspect of what you've written.

4. Think and plan ahead so that you can manage communications well with your candidate peers and the panel.

5. Remember the formality of the situation and however probing, casual or familiar other people are, be careful to ensure a professional and measured response throughout.

If like me, you're thrown, you can easily and quickly remember the strategies you've learnt throughout this book. Now that you've practised the 7/11 Breathing from Chapter 3, you can simply take one deep breath as you listen to the question and relax on the out breadth as you give yourself time to slow down and think.

You can also remember to use your super state anchor to fire off those good feelings in preference to experiencing the agitation, panic or paranoia mentioned above.

With regard to the discussion amongst the interviewees in the waiting room, you can choose to wait elsewhere and/or imagine the candidate who is leading the discussions as a caricature with a silly voice, and notice how your state changes and you want to smile [discretely, of course] when you hear the same words that were previously annoying, singing a new tune!

As you prepare for the formal element of the interview, I'm not going to tell you to listen to the question and answer what they ask because that's something you already know. I am, however, keen that you learn how to speak the same language as your audience.

A few years ago, having seen how our neighbours had remodelled their house [previously a replica of our own] I rushed home to inspire my husband that we should do the same.

"You should see what they've done at number 5...**Imagine** what we can achieve if we knock through this wall to create a new dining space and move the utility into the garage. Let me **illustrate** how we can create more light and storage, and then you can **picture** what I mean." With that, I drew a quick sketch and waited for his reaction, only to be met with a frown!

A few days later, we were coming back from a walk and the neighbours were out gardening. As we got chatting, I recalled, "I've been **telling** Dave all about your 'new' house and was wondering if we can pop in so that he can get a **feel** for what we can **do**."

Moments later, we were inside and suddenly the penny dropped when Dave [my husband] exclaimed, "Wow! It **feels** so spacious. We can **do** this! I'm getting a **sense**; you can really **relax** in here."

As an aspiring teacher, you already know that we process information or think about our world via the senses. When we recall information or express ourselves, we use language that reflects the modality [visual auditory, kinaesthetic, olfactory or gustatory] that it was stored/coded in. 60% of people show a preference for the visual and the remaining 40% recall tend to predominantly recall sounds [auditory] or emotions/feelings [kinaesthetic].

You'll notice from reading my house metaphor above that I use visual predicates [words] and my husband expresses himself through emotional/feeling terms. This gives you a great insight into how you can bring your classroom [now and then] alive for your audience. The activity at the end of this chapter, will support you to create a "real" experience for your audience. Once you've completed this activity, you'll be well rehearsed in looping through the three main sensory modalities [visual, auditory and kinaesthetic]. Be sure to tell the interviewers exactly what they can expect to see, hear and feel in your classroom to give them a flavour of what it would be like to be a student in your class.

If you want to really stand out and give a stellar performance, you can also recall and use the "Future Pace" technique, noted in Chapter 4. Having completed the mock interview in Chapter 6, you'll remember to refer to each of the issues that a question suggests, relate it to your current practice and the impact that you've had to date. As the star candidate, you can then relate your answers to the school's current improvement plan and be clear about what you'll do in your class to raise standards in the school's unique context. Be careful though! If you start using phrases like, "When I take up my post..." you'll sound presumptuous and be unlikely to win hearts. You can be subtle and use sentence starters that convince the panel that you know their context and you're applying with open eyes.

You may say something like, "In order to raise standards in boys writing, a current priority in Key Stage 2, I will also…" This enables the panel to imagine your practice within their setting, and if they can "see" you being successful in their school, they'll be more likely to give your interview serious consideration.

It will also serve you well to be aware that most interview panels follow best practice recruitment guidelines. As such, each panel member is asked to rate each answer numerically. Scores are then combined, and the candidates ranked accordingly, before the panel start their deliberations. This enables the panel to ensure that they are fair and equitable and consider the merits of each candidate when informing their final decision. Your written reference is only taken into account at the point at which they want to offer you the job. This ensures that you are offered the post based on your own credibility and not simply on the back of an influential referee.

Going back to the Chair of Governors who was formerly the boy next door, I recall that when he invited me back into the room after to panel deliberations, I was on my guard to be far more circumspect. I had no idea whether I was on a "call back", and about to be asked a few more questions or whether I was about to be offered the post. I'm pleased to share that it was the latter and I happily accepted based on the terms and conditions agreed. After the formalities, the Chair of Governors noted that I won the hearts of the panel when I referred to a reception child as a "Little Dot"! As Mum of a young lady with Down Syndrome, I remember being a tad surprised when I took up my second headship that children with Special Educational Needs [SEN] in my new school were known as "Bless 'ems"!

You'll remember that I was thrown when asked probing questions about my comments about the environment. When the panel reiterated the question, I realised that they had presupposed that I was talking about relationships in the workplace, rather that the physical aspects of a supportive learning environment. If I hadn't asked them to rephrase the question, I would never have known, and they may have thought I was unable to answer.

And, thinking back to the link inspector who had actively supported me not to talk myself out of a job, I realised in retrospect that after a two-day interview I was starting to flag. Hence, a note to self, was to maintain good energy on interview days thereafter. These days, I use NLP anchoring to recall a time when my energy and focus were good, in order to re-anchor myself back into a resourceful state and you may choose to do the same. You can do this by adding to the Super State anchor that you set in Chapter 9, as well as the 3 Rs – refuelling, rehydrating and reenergising throughout the day. Over recent years, I haven't hesitated to leave the building and take in a walk and some fresh air, throughout an interview day. I've even practise self-hypnosis in my car to be re-energised quickly. Again, I'm not going to tell you what to do because you already know what's right for you.

Re: The Chair of Governors who met me informally over a cup of coffee, I'm now old enough and wise enough to realise that the school were sounding me out regarding my ability to cope with my first baby and my first job all at once. You'll be glad to hear that this is unusual, and most employers are careful to ensure a fair process and equal opportunities for all candidates.

Key Points

Remember to:

★ **Keep your guard up at all times** – All eyes are on you and this is your opportunity to show the whole school community that you're a true professional.

★ **Mind your language** – Be politically correct and show your personality without sailing close to the wind like me.

★ **Calibrate yourself** – notice how you're feeling throughout the day and adjust to maintain high energy and a good emotional state.

★ **Keep your eye on the prize** – Remember how much you want that job of your dreams throughout the process, so that whatever happens you quickly adjust and get yourself back on track!

★ **Remember your "Super-State" anchor and fire it off when you need it most.**

And finally, I hope you've enjoyed your journey to interview and that this introduction to NLP and hypnosis has supported you to prepare well. Now, enjoy treading the boards on your interview stage. To your very best success!

Tanya x

Hypnosis Download

If you would like to purchase the hypnosis download that complements this book:

YOUR TRANCE TO SHINE & GET THE TEACHING JOB YOU WANT

please visit Tanya's website at:

www.tanyabuntingcoaching.org

"Don't close the book and leave the learning behind.
Realise that it's only the beginning of what you
are going to do with the rest of your life."

Dr Richard Bandler

Glossary

Anchor A stimulus that triggers a response, e.g. A particular perfume may trigger a specific memory.

Anchoring The process of associating an internal response with an external stimulus [similar to classical conditioning], so that the response can be re-accessed consciously and sometimes unconsciously.

Auditory Relating to the sense of hearing.

Calibration The process of reading another person's emotional state via their unconscious responses or non-verbal communication cues, including body language, gestures, tone of voice, breathing pattern, and so on

Chunking an experience up to realise the big picture, or down to recognise the details.

Congruence When a person's internal beliefs, values, strategies and behaviours are all aligned.

Future Pacing The process of mentally rehearsing oneself or someone else in the future, in order to ensure that the desired behaviour will occur naturally and automatically.

Kinaesthetic Relation to body sensations, feeling and movement.

Limiting Belief A belief that stops someone from reaching their goals.

Metaphor A story, parable or an analogy.

Rapport The presence of trust, harmony and co-operation within a relationship.

State The ongoing mental and physical conditions from which a person is acting,

Visual Relation to the sense of seeing.

Further Reading

To further support your well-being and development through your teaching career:

Bandler, R. and Benson, K., 2018, *Teaching Excellence: The Definitive Guide to NLP for Teaching and Learning (NLP for Education)*, New Thinking Publications

Bandler, R. and La Valle, J., *Persuasion Engineering: Sales & Business Language and Behaviour*, Meta Publications Inc.

Bandler, R. and Thomason, G., *The Secrets of Being Happy*, I.M. Press, Inc.

Cooke, K., *Happy Brain: Using Play, Creativity and NLP to Supercharge Your Child's Thrive Drive*, Balboa.Press, 2020

How to Ask Tanya for Help

Get the Teaching Job You Want was written because more and more teachers were requesting Tanya's Personal & Career Coaching Skills.

To access individual or group coaching with Tanya, either face to face or on Zoom, contact her via her website at:

www.tanyabuntingcoaching.org

Tanya Bunting Coaching
Hypnotherapy and NLP

If you want to become a Licensed Practitioner of NLP via The Society of NLP, Tanya will be happy to discuss how you can start your NLP journey and develop these skills within the classroom and beyond.